Teaching the Actor Craft

By Jon Jory

TEACHING THE ACTOR CRAFT

By Jon Jory

SMITH AND KRAUS PUBLISHERS   2013

Teaching the Actor Craft Copyright © 2013 Jon Jory

All rights reserved. This book is fully protected under the copyright laws of the United States of America and of all countries covered by the International Copyright Union (including the Dominion of Canada and the rest of the British Commonwealth), The Berne Convention, the Pan-American Copyright Convention and the Universal Copyright Convention as well as all countries with which the United States has reciprocal copyright relations. All rights, including professional/amateur stage rights, motion picture, recitation, lecturing, public reading, radio broadcasting, television, video or sound recording, all other forms of mechanical or electronic reproduction, such as CD-ROM, CD-I, DVD, information storage and retrieval systems and photocopying, and the rights of translation into foreign languages, are strictly reserved.

All rights reserved.

ISBN: 1-57525-792-0
ISBN: 978-1-57525-792-1
Library of Congress Control Number: 2012956533

Typesetting and layout by Elizabeth E. Monteleone
Cover Design by Elizabeth E. Monteleone
Cover photography © Sergey Nivens–fotalia.com

A Smith and Kraus book
177 Lyme Road, Hanover, NH 03755
Editorial 603.643.6431 To Order 1.800.558.2846
www.smithandkraus.com

Printed in the United States of America

Dedication

For Marcia my wife.

*For my remarkable and loved children,
Jessica, Victor and Miranda.*

For my excellent sister, Jean.

*For my friends and mavens of theatre,
Michael Dixon, Alan Cook and Mark Jenkins.*

*For my comrades of the long march: Sandy Speer,
Trish Pugh, Marilee Herbert Slater, Paul Owen, Adale
O'Brien, William McNulty, Wanda Snyder, Debra Monk,
James Roemer, Jeff Rodgers, V. Craig Heidenreich,
Buzz and Roanne Victor.*

*For the one who left the table too early,
Susan Kingsley.*

For all the wonderful actors who taught me this book.

*For the remarkable philanthropists who made the
illogical possible, Mr. and Mrs. Bingham Senior,
Barry Bingham, Jr., Owsley Brown, and David Jones.*

*And the people I wanted to be:
Victor Jory, Charles Lane, Tyrone Guthrie, Elia Kazan,
Lazlo Marton, Michael Langham, and Ann Bogart.*

I know, get the hook.

Contents

What is the Actor's Craft?   9
Teaching Craft   11
What is the Student Experience in
   Learning Craft?   12
Warning   12

The Physical

Physicalizing the Transition   17
Focus Points   21
Torque   25
Still/Movement/Still   29
Vacillation   34
Changing Architecture   42
Intentional and Intuitive Gesture   47
Held Gesture/Controlled Drop   51
Three Gestures   53
The Helicopter   56

The Verbal

The Run-On Sentence   59
Spreading the Line   65
Breaking Up the Line   69
Framing the Line   73
Throwing the Line Away   76
Closing it Down   79
The Cut Line   84
The Greater Overlap   90
The Lesser Overlap   93
Lifting   96
The Unwritten Interjection   100
Flat   105

THE RHYTHM
   Rhythm Blocks 113
   Shared Rhythm   116
   The Quick Park   121
   The Slow Part   125
   The Pause   128
   Beats as Rhythm   139
   The Build   143
   Lay On/Lay Off   148

DOING THINGS
   Behavior   154
   Clean and Dirty   160
   Small, Medium, Big   172
   Props in Eight   176
   Choreographing Behavior   182
   The Illusion of the First Time   188
   Taking the Arrow   191
   Setup/Joke/Reaction   195
   Handling the Prop   198
   Detail   201
   Doing Nothing   204
   The False Exit   207
   Sounds   211
   The Double Take   215
   Giving and Taking the Eyes   218
   Ripples from the Big Moment   222

COURSE STRUCTURES
   Outline for Teaching Beginning Craft   231
   Outline for Teaching Advanced Craft   232
   If Only One Course is Taught   233
   Acting Craft for High Schools   234

COMBINATION EXERCISES
    Combos   235
    Combo Speech #1   236
    Combo Speech #2   237
    Combo Speech #3   238
    Combo Speech #4   240
    Combo Speech #5   242
    Combo Speech #6   243

Afterword   245

WHAT IS CRAFT?

The house of acting is supported by six pillars: text analysis, the voice, physicality, psychology, emotion, and craft. These pillars are rooted by the imagination and floored by the text. These elements are interdependent, an ecology, but necessarily are taught separately and then reunited in productions. In acting curriculums, I find classes in all these disciplines (emotion and psychology are usually taught through acting systems), except for craft. Why? Craft is the delivery system for mind and heart. At NASA, the payloads mean little if you can't get them up in the air.

Craft is composed of dozens of learnable and even mechanical skills that make manifest the imagination and reveal the text. How do you use props to give focus and make points? How do you "throw away" one line to give extra value to the next? How is rhythm used to parse the script and sustain interest? What is a "build" and why does one employ it? What exactly is a "double take" and why should you care? What are the values and limits of "pace"? How do you "frame a line," "tag an act," use "overlap," and "clean up" a sit?

Until the '80s, these techniques were learned by young actors steadily in rehearsal and performance with vastly more experienced older actors. When resident companies, touring straight plays and professional stock companies declined, the young actors moved to training programs, working mainly with other young actors of shared inexperience. "Methods" were taught that addressed in some part the voice, the body, the psychology and emotion (and to a lesser degree, text analysis) while craft was deemed less important and in a few cases, disdained. The elephant was now missing a leg.

Emotion must be partnered by craft to avoid indulgence. Honesty and truth need to hold stage. Psychology needs craft to be understood. Craft, not being theoretical, is difficult to mine from acting methods or closed systems. Try teaching the double take by using sense memory and given circumstances.

Craft is, obviously, only one of the six pillars of acting, and only a fool would consider it an end in itself, but it is crucial to the other five. It is, however, a necessary discipline and thus deserves, in fact demands, a place in acting's architecture. Hopefully this book will contribute to bringing craft more directly into the room where acting is taught.

TEACHING CRAFT

There are various scenarios at the end of the book for the teaching of craft in a university or high school setting. The exercises may also be scattered through acting, scene study, and style courses. Included are fifty categories with exercises and coaching tips under each heading.

The exercises are brief monologues and dialogues written for the particular skill being taught. These may be learned by the students the night before, or in the first ten minutes of the class, thus assuring that the dog hasn't eaten anyone's homework. The brevity of the exercises allows the teacher to get a maximum number of actors on their feet and working each session. Repetition of each exercise is key. First, get it, than repeat it.

Ideally, each class should come prepared with audition pieces, and a simple scene should be chosen and learned by all. These are used for further practice with the techniques and for review of several techniques at one time. In class, after three categories have been studied and performed, I assign all three to be shown together, which is universally enjoyed and promotes learning. I also return to key techniques for review and use the combination exercises to increase the level of difficulty before the class disbands.

If these fifty categories are employed to teach a beginning and then advanced craft class, there should be easily enough work for a full year. If scattered through a more general curriculum, they should serve the student throughout a multi-year stay.

Craft classes have been enormously popular with students who love achieving mastery and can see progress on a daily basis.

Bon Voyage.

WHAT IS THE STUDENT EXPERIENCE IN LEARNING CRAFT?

Forgive me a story. Growing up, I had good hand-eye coordination and taught myself a decent game of tennis without taking lessons. A friend, Danny Newcomb, from down the street lost to me steadily until he spent the summer with a local pro, learned the mechanics of serve and a backhand, and returned to whip me unmercifully. Chagrined, I resorted to the pro, who schooled my non-existent technique. The first thing that happened was that my natural game fell apart. Learning the proper strokes, I now felt self-conscious and longed for the day when I "just played." The second thing that happened was that over the months I got worlds better, regained some holistic focus, and joyfully returned to taking Danny apart. So it is with learning the actor's craft.

As you begin, you go through a stage where you can't see the forest for the trees. Your work may feel robotic and short sighted. You can't just "play the game," you can only think about your "backhand." Persevere. When technique is fully absorbed (and it will be) through repetition, it becomes spontaneous. You no longer think about it; it just is. Keep working until you're no longer aware of working. At that point, your acting improves exponentially.

WARNING

Craft (or technique) used without integrating the other five pillars of acting is the devil's handiwork.

The other five pillars, absent craft, make terrible soup.

REPETITION. In teaching craft I have mentioned the necessity of repetition. Craft exercises are easy to understand but hard to embody. It's not just doing it 'right' that teaches. It's doing it 'right' several times. This is hard on both teacher and student because...well, it's boring. I fight my impulse to move on and do it again. I have also found that every three or four classes it's best to spend a class repeating exercises they did three weeks ago (or more). It's better to end up doing fewer exercises and giving more repetition. That way some of the work will actually show up in performance. I know how hard it is to do it once more when the students already think they've nailed it. Understanding is one thing, absorption another.

THE PHYSICAL

PHYSICALIZING THE TRANSITION

The transition occurs when we move from one want to another want or one subject to another subject. For instance:

      Jack
This is over. I don't ever want to see you again. Never. Ever.

(Transition)

And you're not taking the dog, you understand that?

Or as in:

      Jill
What do I care about the dog? This isn't about pets, okay, this is about us.

(Transition)

And don't nod at me. It's patronizing. You think the dog is my concern?

USAGE
 Something has to get the actor from subject one to subject two. Sometimes it is thought and sometimes it is thought plus something physical. *The advantage of physicalizing the transition is that it makes the bridge from one idea to the next visual as well as mental.* In the following exercise, seat the actor in a chair and have the actor make the transition physically. Insist on the three repetitions. The first time have

17

the actor crosses her or his legs as the transitional moment. The second time the actor will look up at the ceiling and then back out at the audience. The third time the actor will rub their hands together. Let's try it.

EXERCISE

A
The woman was dead, I knew that the moment I saw her.

(Transition)

Do you have a cup of coffee, I need the caffeine.

COACHING

Have each actor do the three repetitions one right after the other using the different physicalities. Remind them that there needs to be thought as well as the physical. Once every actor has done the three repetitions, go around again, using the same lines, but have the actor invent the physicality to go with the transitional moment. In my experience, the actors immediately get it and see its value. Now have the actors pair off and do this short scene physicalizing the transitions.

A
So you're saying the guy stole the money.

(Transition)

Come on, pay attention to me.

B
How am I supposed to know? I'm not like a professional crime solver.

(Transition)

Can we just forget this for tonight?

A
No. He could hop in a car, leave the state.

(Transition)

Man, I have a splitting headache.
B
There's aspirin in the drawer to the left of the sink.

(Transition)

How much was there that he got?

COACHING
When the actors perform the duologue, it is your call whether the physicality chosen seems to fit the characters and the circumstances: if you feel it does not, have them re-do the exercise immediately, using different physicalities. Most acting problems in the exercises will disappear by the third repetition. Ah, the mysterious power of three! The physicality is not simply random, it expresses the character's emotional state in physical terms. Basic circumstances must be set by the actors before they can perform the exercise. Who are these people? Where are they? What is their relationship? What are the "wants"? Now let each actor choose the transitions and physicalize them in a short monologue.

A
It was… I don't know… pretty creepy. It was pitch black out there. You couldn't see two feet in front of you, plus the battery went dead in my flashlight. I can't even describe the sound. It was as if something fell. Big noise. I ran. Got out of there. You think I should have stuck around, right?

COACHING
There is no point in the class arguing about where each actor placed the transitions unless they seem really random. Don't let them get away with placing a transition after every

line, however. If the transitions are unclear, ask the actor to name them and then do the exercise again. This is a good exercise to allow a second actor as the listener. The exercise can, with value, be done again, keeping the transition placement but changing the physicality. If they do it the first time sitting, make the second try standing or lying. The exercise can also be done again using a prop like a cup of coffee or an activity such as getting a splinter out with a needle. *Many young actors feel awkward physically and the structure of identifying transitions and physicalizing them increases their sense of ease and concentration.*

Focus Points

Here is the antidote to looking eternally into the other actor's eyes (terminal eye lock) or playing without surcease to a point centrally located out over the audiences' heads. The focus points for the actor are:
1) to the left
2) to the center
3) to the right
4) up to the ceiling
5) down to the floor
6) behind you.

Basic Exercise

The class may stay where they are and you call out the six focus points. You do the little military drill in order a couple of times and then randomly in a sort of theatrical Simon Says.

A change of focus is tied to, and makes manifest, thought process. It physicalizes what the mind conceives and ends up being a useful behavior. First, let's play with it in monologue form.

Usage

As usual, we'll begin with an enforced pattern. Where the actor looks is made clear in the exercise in the form of stage directions. The actors should, once again, learn that this isn't the "right" way to do the pieces. It is an illustration of how focus point might be used.

Exercise

A

(Looking out center over the audience.)

Hi, I'm Randy's date.

(Looks down.)

Date to be actually. Date du jour. Date a la carte.

(Looks to the left.)

Set up by the overbearing mother. Mine, to clarify.

(Looks behind. Looks back center.)

Keeping it down because overbearing mother is in the next room.

(Looks at ceiling.)

There will be no end to this. These dates will proceed inexorably 'til the mountains are dust heaps.

(Looks out center again.)

Which is the subject of our two hours traffic of the stage.

Coaching

Obviously, this is a direct address soliloquy. We are also overstating the change of focus by having it fall only at sentence end. Still, the result makes clear the usefulness of the technique. It is lifelike in the sense that we naturally adjust our focus while speaking and thinking. What is not lifelike is the obsessive staring in one place that often occurs in acting. How long should focus be held before changing? Would that one could say, but that depends utterly on the circumstances, the character, and the necessities of text. What we can say, with confidence is that it increases believability and gives thought a physical dimension. Also, the look up at the ceiling, down at the floor, and the look behind you are underused and thus benefit the actor and the moment because of rarity. When the above exercise is performed, remind the actor to actually see what they look at. Let's try an actor's choice exercise where the focus points, frequency, and where they fall (not always on the punctuation) are all performer's choice.

Exercise

A

(Sitting while actor B moves around setting a table for four.)
Jim's going to be… what is Jim going to be, let's say embarrassed, when he and Carol arrive, because he knows we know while Carole doesn't know. Which only goes to prove that friendship cannot service negative info and we should all be very, very careful about… well, let's call it "messing around."

B

Yeah and choosing to mess around with a lunatic who wanders around carving hearts in trees. What on Earth could that girl be thinking? Someone should impound her pocket knife. Carol goes to that park, okay, someday she'll lean against the wrong tree and you can kiss that marriage goodbye. This is conceivably going to be the worst dinner party of the decade.

Usage

Every point of focus need not be used, but let's say each actor uses four of the six. Remember the focus change can be in the middle of the line. A focus change can occur with equal value while the other person is speaking. Because the audience will often look where the actor looks, we seldom spend the entire time looking away from the speaker. As a set of rules for the above exercise, most of the focus changes should occur when speaking. Some changes can be used more than once (looking left, etc). The actor could also combine changes (looks down, looks right, looks behind, speaks).

Coaching

The change of focus can be emotional, as in: The actor looks at the ground not to see a beetle but because of embarrassment. It can be specific, as in: The actor looks down to see if he remembered to shine his shoes. He may also look to the left to avoid someone's eyes. Obviously, this exercise is related to "giving and taking the eyes" elsewhere in this book. You may have to encourage the look at the ceiling and the look behind. They seem more exotic to the actors. Remind them that this is seldom something we sit at home planning. Focus is best when it is spontaneous, however moments of planned focus change are far from unusual. This exercise bears repetition so the actors can play with the idea.

It will also serve to have the actors reverse the roles. It's also useful to have them do this work with an audition piece they have been using. It will, in most cases, change the piece for the better and validate the concept. You may have to say, "You fulfilled the terms of the exercise, but I don't believe the mental process. Let's see it again."

TORQUE

What is it? *It's a sudden explosion of physical energy, perhaps, but not always, accompanied by vocal explosiveness as well.* Think of the drag racer sitting quietly at the starting line and then the sudden roaring and screeching off the start. If we want a stage image, see a woman seated at a table after her husband's false accusations, which she has born in silence. She is looking down, her hands folded, she seems almost relaxed in the face of the verbal barrage. Suddenly, her hand flashes out, sweeping a vase, her coffee cup, and a honey jar onto the floor. That's torque. It's a sudden split-second move from stillness to powerful action. If the torque is mainly vocal, it just as suddenly shatters the quiet. What are these moments psychologically? They are the release of strong feelings, which may have been restrained but can no longer be contained. These feelings can range from joy to rage, but they break through relative calm much as the electric light flashes on the flip of a switch. *Torque is a sudden jump from normalcy to extreme.* Can it be accompanied by text? Of course, but it needn't be. It depends on the actor, the script, and the circumstances. Let's try a couple.

EXERCISE
Building on what we said above, a man or a woman sits at table. The other character verbally attacks. Where you find the (1) sign, the person at the table explodes physically, but the physicality does not extend. Like a flash of lightning, it is there then is gone. The actor should choose the physical nature of the explosion. The verbal attacker should be far enough from the table not to be struck by hands or objects. The speech continues after the explosion, but is, of course, affected by it.

A

You think you have complete freedom of action, right? You do what you do independent of anybody's feelings or needs. It's your universe and the rest of us are your creatures gratefully accepting whatever you dish out. And the craziest thing is, you think we should be grateful. Well, that's over. I'm through with that. Don't call me. You understand? Do-not-call-me.

COACHING

In using torque, the teacher will have to give some examples, such as standing suddenly, slapping the table, punching the air, etc. The duration of the explosion can vary. Usually, it continues until self-control reasserts itself after a few seconds. It is not a thought out reaction or should certainly not appear so. It has nothing to do with the physical violence wreaked on another person. It is the body and voice suddenly releasing pent-up or triggered response. It is the speed of the change from nothing to something that counts here. If the actor is asked to repeat the exercise with the same text, they should change the physicality. Is the actor capable of not planning the response but trusting that a spontaneous response will be there? This is a particularly good exercise for people who have a somewhat slower metabolism. Now let's try an exercise where the speaker experiences the torqued moment. In the first example, the moment is underlined.

EXERCISE

A

I took it all. Everything he said and he said a lot. He said a lot. And I sat there. I sat there and I didn't move.

USAGE

The torqued moment can be very brief. It's often off a piece of punctuation rather than continuing through an entire line. As I will often remind this book's reader, all technique exercises are based on the use of given circumstances that the actor using this text must create. The exercises for torque may be done sitting, standing, lying, or moving. Here's another one with the torqued moment left to the discretion of the actor.

EXERCISE
A
God, I am so incredibly, dizzyingly happy. I cannot believe it worked out this way. Did I see this coming? Not in a million years.

USAGE
These brief exercises can be done with only a single actor but done by two or three actors on stage it allows the listeners an opportunity to react to a big moment. Young or inexperienced actors often let someone else's big moment pass with out recognizing it is a golden moment for them as well. Here's a dual exercise; each actor should find one torqued moment.

EXERCISE
A
What the hell is going on here? You moved the furniture again? This isn't an art installation, this is where we live. Sometimes after a rough day I like to walk in here and find the damn sofa where I left it. What's the impetus for this? What?

B
I don't like same, okay? Same partner, same house, same car, same job. And, now that you bring it up, same furniture. You're like the perfect candidate for a life sentence. You'd find the cell comforting.

COACHING
Many actors have never ever moved that fast, not even for a split second. Some actors trying the exercise will need several repetitions just to get this idea into their muscles

and memory systems. You must push them to increase the physical speed of the moment. Torque, in one sense, is an extreme. Because the exercises are brief, you can probably give the students at least three repetitions. Make sure, given that the asked for movement is emotional as well as physical, that the moment comes out of a state that could have produced it. In a few cases, the torque could appear without emotional preparation. For instance: A woman sits reading a magazine, relaxed, feet up. Another woman enters and says, "The dog's been killed." The seated woman immediately throws the magazine against the wall, hard. There's torque without preparation.

Still/Movement/Still

There is a lot of "still" taught in the American theatre as in, "Just stand there and do it," or, "We don't need the extraneous 'acting'." All of this is useful and it recognizes the power of stillness which is a reality. *What it fails to include is that the power of stillness, is magnified at the moment it becomes movement, and the power of movement is increased at the moment it becomes stillness.* "Still" is often easier for the actor once they get into it. The young actor will often feel safer, and will in fact be better, at stillness than at movement. The problem is that the stillness becomes a default position rather than a charged moment. The best stillness is gathering to act, not retreat. The point of the set of exercises, however, is to learn to couple movement and stillness and thus empower and define the text. The first exercise starts with the actor sitting completely still then getting up and moving in the underlined section and returning to absolute stillness thereafter.

Exercise
   A
   There were six of them in the square. They just appeared, you didn't see them coming. They all carried bats, or pipe or two-by-fours. Once they were there, you couldn't get out. *Why the hell didn't I yell at her, tell her to run? What was wrong with me?* They beat her until she wasn't moving anymore. Then they just turned around and walked off. Left her.

Usage

The stillness should be longing for release. The movement should be the body releasing. The actor should fully commit to both. The transitional moment from one to the other should be driven by the actor's mind and feelings. Why move? Why be still? The key, however, is that the piece contains both. The actors need to learn the necessity of both.

Coaching

The actor may need purposeful movement. By that I mean you might suggest they take off their coat and throw it on the floor. Or they open the fridge and take out a cake and slam it on the table. It makes the transition from stillness to movement and back easier for the actor to handle. Perhaps the second time through you might stipulate that the movement be more clearly "emotional" and less behavioral. They may struggle, but it's worth it. Telling them they are on the right track but you want to see another repetition will usually improve their work. Now let's do two exercises where the actor chooses the textual time to break the stillness and return to it.

Exercise

A

Incredible. Where was my mind? How many hours a day, year after year after year, did I spend with him? And where was I that I didn't understand the guy was a racist? Full blown. Way, way out there. My father with a closet full of guns and a shoebox full of ammunition. How many things are there that are right in front of us and we never see? How many?

Exercise

A

So she says, "You're not going to believe this. Come out front." And I do, and she's got this little trailer thing hitched to that beat-up Jeep. In the trailer is a lioness. She has this humongous beast out front of my house. Then she asks me if I want her? This is a person I knew from my book club. You can't tell a book by its cover, right?

USAGE
We've already said that you give the actor between five and ten minutes to learn the speech. It's best they don't carry the paper when they present the exercise, but if working with someone for whom quick memorization is a real issue, just cut them the slack. Hopefully you are in a large enough room that the students can wander about learning and saying the lines. If not, and it is feasible, allow them to go outside the room for the memorization period. *I have found that before they present, they need to have said the exercise full voice.* Otherwise, actually hearing their own voice as they present can shatter their concentration.

COACHING
Always praise when possible and laugh when the inevitable mistakes occur after such short preparation. If you have already practiced the torque technique, it can be helpfully combined with this exercise. If stillness is awkward for a standing actor (many look as if they're being punished), sit them down. Slight movement is absolutely all right inside stillness. Too much rigor will just scare the actor. Because the exercise speeches are short, I usually ask them to begin again when they forget the line. It's better that they fully experience the exercise in a gulp. After each actor does the exercise, I usually simply say, "Thank you," and move on. If you correct or praise, try to draw a conclusion from it. Think of it not as a criticism but as a teaching moment. If someone is really having trouble with an exercise, ask if you may skip past them for the moment. If you do, ask them if they would like to go again once the others have finished. Often I ask the actor to do it again without saying why, *based on my knowledge that repetition is usually more responsible for improvement than the teacher's theory.* Here's a duologue exercise for "still to movement to still."

Exercise

It might be helpful to have one actor do "still, movement, still" and the other do "movement, still, movement." Then, if there is time, reverse.

A
What is that over there?
B
What? Where? You mean the bridge?

A
Is that a guy on the railing? Is that part of the bridge or is that a guy?

B
You think that's a jumper?

A
Yeah. What else would that be? Call 911.

B
I don't have my phone.

A
He went.

B
Oh my God. Did we see that? The guy just killed himself. What do we do?

A
Nothing to do. What would there be to do?

Coaching

Make sure each actor has all three elements in place. Was the movement enough to make the stillness stand out? Were both states believable? Did the stillness seem forced or inevitable when performed? Sometimes I will use class time to have one pair do several repetitions of the exercise. How did the piece develop? What did the acting gain from repetition? If it was not done on a bare stage, do that next. What drives the behavior in that case? If the actors are enjoying and benefitting, then reverse the roles, give them give minutes for study, and then do another round of performance. The point is to become aware of how physical variety deepens the work and makes it more interesting.

VACILLATION

Start one way, decide against it, go another way. That's almost as clear a definition as we need. We sometimes get too much clarity in the blocking. Jim rises from his chair, goes directly to the refrigerator, gets a Dr. Pepper, goes directly back to chair, sits. What's wrong with that? Nothing if that's what happens some of the time. A lot if that's what happens all of the time. *The most direct path isn't always the most interesting visually or psychologically.*

Let's look at Jim again. He starts to get up to go to the fridge and realizes the beautiful and judgmental Lydia will be arriving. He doesn't think she'll cotton to the idea of him knocking back Dr. Pepper at 9 a.m. A moment later, he decides that's ridiculous and gets up heading for the fridge. On his way, he remembers he left his wallet somewhere, maybe it's in the bathroom. He starts to divert. He puts his hand on the fridge door and stands lost in thoughts of the decisive Lydia. After three or four seconds, he opens the fridge and gets the drink. Heads back to chair. Oops, left fridge door open. Goes back, closes it. Goes to chair. Sits. That's vacillation. Or we can call it interrupted behavior or constantly revised thought process made visible. Whatever, the point is that too much physical movement on the stage is completely predictable to the viewer. Or, dare we say, boring? Vacillation can be as simple as reaching to take off your glasses and in the midst of the movement to do so, changing your mind and leaving them on. It acknowledges that our physical life is messy as well as clean. Acting that always takes the most direct route seems un-lifelike. In the following exercise, please follow the given blocking slavishly.

Exercise
   A
   I know you weren't looking forward to this *(shows a physical impulse to rise but restrains it half done and stays sitting)*, Dan *(rises)*... I just *(turns to move away. Turns back)*... I'm sorry. I want to wish you well. *(Starts to put out hand, decides against it.)* Your check is already at reception. *(Starts to exit. Turns back to speak. Doesn't speak. Exits.)*

Usage
   Odd as it may seem, have each class member do this exercise exactly as written.

Coaching
   Make sure they do the blocking as written. No further blocking or vacillations should be added. When the actor turns to move away then turns back, there shouldn't be a full stop involved. The thought that changes the movements should take place in the midst of the movement. Vacillation in the way we are defining it implies in-motion changes. It doesn't mean "Turns away. Stops. Thinks. Turns back." It means "Turn away. In the midst of the turn, turn back."

Usage
   Vacillation can be minute or very much full body. It can be behavioral as in going to get the Dr. Pepper, or it can be impulse driven as in, "I start to stretch. I don't." Now try a speech in which you find your own examples of vacillations.

Exercise
   A
   It was kinda funny. No, it really was. He's still got on the gorilla suit from the gig but he ducks into this golf store to see how this new putter handles. There was a plate glass window and six or seven people are standing out there watching a gorilla putt. Anyway, it was funnier than you think it was.

Coaching

Remember it's best if the vacillation interrupts before the action is completed. If the actor mimes a putt, the vacillation interrupts before the mime is completed. Council moderation. The exercise doesn't demand six examples of vacillations. Two or three will do quite nicely. Some actors live to use technique exercises to demonstrate wild, untrammeled creativity and eccentricity. The exercises are usually better fulfilled by using moderation and simple belief. Of course, a few classroom laughs are worth their weight in gold. I don't believe I've mentioned before that it's good for the actors if they are never consistently last or consistently first in doing them. I usually say I have a number between one and ten (or however many there are in class), and go down the line until someone hits it and then they go. Try another exercise.

Exercise

A
So, I just want to get this straight—you never said it? Because I'm going to believe what you say, so there's a responsibility here. I'm going to act out of faith and I will hope that faith is not misplaced.

B
You know, I hear what you're saying but mainly I hear how you say it and the how doesn't sound like somebody who has my best interest at heart. The how sounds skeptical, maybe a little vengeful. I'm surprised by "how" you say that.

Coaching

It is very often a sudden, unanticipated burst of emotion that makes us vacillate. The burst of emotion kind of knocks us off one path and sets us on another. See if the actors can find that as the root cause is a physical change of direction. By the way, keep remembering to remind the actors that they need to create the circumstances that surround each exercise. In the one above, you can't really place the exchange without imagining what "B" said immediately previously. *The teacher needs to have the actors articulate, in brief, the circumstances they are using before they proceed.*

Usage
    To assist vacillation, the architecture of the space needs to be clean. The door is where and leads to what? Outside the window is what? They are in a junkyard, a meadow, or a forest? The actors should quickly explain the architecture before they begin.

ANCILLARY ACTION

This is adding the elements of a simple, clear, achievable task as a physical structure for a scene or monologue. The elements of said task organize, inform, enlighten, and add believability to the text (and, may I say, to the actor's disarrayed mind). So here's how it goes. The famous example is the shoe exercise. During the following monologue, the actor puts on a sock, puts on a shoe, finishes lacing it, ties the bow, and stands up on the final sentence of the monologue. Okay, let's do a shoe. The commentary is simple to show the way it could be done.

A

Okay, someone comes up to you on a street.

(Sits on floor)

They got a lottery ticket. A winner.

(Pulls out sock)

They can't cash it 'cause they're an illegal immigrant.

(Picks up shoe)

Wants you to cash it; you split the money. That's the 'shimmy.'

(Laces the shoelace)

Woman comes up, overhears, says it's a good idea. Everybody should put up a hundred dollars faith money.

(Stops lacing)

She's the Switch.

(Continues lacing)

Money goes in an envelope. You hold it. The Switch goes to cash the ticket. The shimmy disappears.

(Puts on shoe)

You look in the envelope. Cut up newspaper.

(Looks up)

You start screamin'—you're out a hundred dollars.

(Ties shoe)

That's the shag, the grift, the hustle.

(Stands up)

That's my job, okay?

USAGE

The speech should be given for memorization the night before. The first time through (they have prepared this), they score the speech exactly as I have done. On the second go-round, they invent a task-score.

COACHING

Make sure they deliver the speech clearly so the activity leaves the speech intact. Oh, and have everybody wear lace-up shoes. It's going to take people a couple of tries, so the first go-round could take longer than one class period. I've chosen an informational speech because it's easier to manage. Emotion doesn't make this work harder it just means the task has to fit spontaneously inside the feelings. Try to get the action to finish the task just in time to stand up for the last line. The benefits are that actor fear declines and believability increases. It also gives the speech shape and gives the work physical dimension. Now, do it again with the actor making their own shape. Counsel them to keep what you consider the perfect moments free of physical activity. Here is a brief list of ancillary tasks.

1) Make tea, pour tea, add lemon and sugar, drink tea.
2) Wash, dry, and put away dishes (this could be mimed, though it adds a level of difficulty).
3) Make a bed.
4) Take out wallet, go through wallet, throw out unnecessary cards, put wallet back.
5) Dig a hole, plant a bulb, cover bulb, smooth earth.
6) Take out knife, sharpen knife, test knife, replace.
7) Make up your own.

The next exercise is a dialogue with each actor having a separate task.

Usage

Have the actors chose tasks suitable to apartment living. Tasks must be completable by the time the dialogue is complete.

Coaching

Make sure the actor's thought process is present inside the task. Is the way they are handling the tasks affected by the emotional undercurrent? Point out that a great part of the acting value lies in their "attitude" toward the task. Have them articulate the "attitude." If it doesn't seem suitable suggest or ask for another. If you think of a workable task and can provide the props, do so. Real props are infinitely more valuable to the exercise. What you hope for in acquainting students with "ancillary" action is that they seek such tasks when they might be suitable to the scene, speech, and play. These are not ideas that only the director may have, achievable tasks build belief, create a physical side of the work, relax the actor, and provide recognizable structure that informs the words an even provokes emotion. If you find this work is helpful and engages your actor, you could have them pick different asks (or simply exchange) and do the above exercise again.

P.S. As usual, you may want to "background" or "back story" the above scene before it is performed.

Changing the Architecture

In this case, we are talking about "architecture" as the way the actor is sitting or standing or lying. This architecture of the body is also seen in relation to chairs, sofas, doorways, walls, and so on. Thank you, Ann Bogart. *It is useful to realize that in all theatre, even that which is the most realistic, the traditional living room or kitchen play has a visual aspect.* Part of that visual aspect is the human body.

Often while listening or talking, while we sit in an armchair or simply stand, we eventually exhaust the viewer's interest and at that imaged point we need to change the "architecture" of our body. It's simple really. A woman stands listening to her brother while he describes a mountain climbing experience. She stands at rest, hands unaffectedly at her sides, taking in this tale of adventure. After a while, perhaps for her own comfort, she folds her arms over her chest. There, she has changed her architecture. A little while later, she shifts her weight and puts her hands behind her back. She has changed her architecture. The net effect is realistic. Changing the architecture is, in the simplest way, theatrical.

Exercise
A man sits on a couch or chair. A woman stands nearby listening.

Man	Woman
So, we were on the ledge. We couldn't go back, we couldn't go down. We were stuck.	
	(Changes architecture.)
(Change of architecture.)	
We could hear the rain coming. It started maybe a half mile off. We knew we had maybe a half-hour of light.	*(Changes architecture.)*
(Changes architecture.)	*(Changes architecture.)*
The guy I was climbing with… I'll never forget this, starts to cry. What could I say to him? We both knew it was finished. We could only be there. I don't know how long it was… Long. Then we heard the chopper.	
(Changes architecture.)	

USAGE

Obviously, the number of changes is arbitrary. Could be more, could be fewer. Might not happen at all. You will see, however, how it assists in keeping the scene alive. Now have the two actors reverse positions. The standing actor (Man or Woman) sits and does the speech. Have them, again, use the written score of when the changes occur. Now do the scene again, re-scoring the changes again for themselves. The coaching might suggest two changes apiece, not more.

Coaching

Remind the actors the changes needn't be huge or eccentric, but they need to be visible. The changes are, of course, psychologically based as well as physical. Encourage them that their work increases visual interest. Keep them to the score. Have them repeat the exercise more than once using different architecture. Make the point that the goal is for this to become second nature rather than planned. *As in all technique exercises, the thought process of the character must be present throughout.*

Exercise

Using the same text, have them abandon the above score and find their own moments for the changes. Keep this new exercise a two character scene.

Coaching

Tell the actors if the changes seem artificial or mechanical. Remind them to keep the scene as realistic as possible. Tell them if they are attempting more changes than the material can bear. Do not spend too long on a single pair. Remember that the work needs to be experienced and we want to get as many people as possible up and working in the class period.

Exercise (Open Stage)

Still using the text of the original exercise, remove the furniture so the work may take place on an empty stage. This is useful because young actors often cling to the furniture so as to feel less vulnerable. The actor will find that the changes in architecture will give a sense of emotional safety (as the furniture did) and encourage a freedom in the acting.

Coaching

Insist they maintain contact with each other during the exercise. You might remind them of the technique of physicalizing transitions, which can deepen the exercises and help them use the empty space. Again, warn them against simply "physically busy."

Exercise

We will close this work with a short duologue used to continue the work on architecture.

A
Excuse me. I just wanted to tell you I enjoyed your lecture. I don't mean to keep you.

B
No problem. You're not keeping me. I didn't catch your name?

A
_____ *(different, of course, if it is a male or female speaking).* You were very… dynamic, self-confident, well-spoken. I liked watching you. It just didn't make much sense.

B
Really? I can't tell if you're joking. You're not joking. I do this a hundred times a year; nobody ever said it didn't make sense.

A
They wouldn't. It would be rude. But I thought someone should… Well, say it… Tell you. It's not possible to talk about "fate" and then assume free will, for instance…

B
Could I just say one thing?

A
Of course.

B
Get lost.

Usage

Once the work becomes a duologue, each character can (and should) change architecture both when speaking and listening. One of each might be useful the first time the exercise is done. I would suggest that the duologue be repeated with and without furniture. Where the changes fall should, at this point, be left to the actor.

Coaching

You could use the idea of "offense" and "defense." *When is an actor attacking, and when defending?* How does that effect the placement and nature of the changes? If an actor is repeating architecture previously used or has trouble with the concept, I sometimes stop the exercise and say to the actor, "Change the architecture each time I clap my hands." The actor usually does this easily a half dozen times, proving they really have no problem.

A Final Word on Architecture

You may be asked if this can be used in rehearsal and performance? Yes. It is basically a training technique but can be of particular help early in rehearsal. It can be used in performance to freshen frozen or locked down moments without essentially changing the scene.

INTENTIONAL AND INTUITIVE GESTURE

Let's say, for the sake of argument, that there are only two sorts of gestures. The first we will call "intuitive" and this category includes all the abstract movements stimulated by our thought process and delivered through the nervous system to our hands, arms, and beyond. The character is unaware of this gestural vocabulary and its energy is both metabolic and situational. We may gesture wildly in a state of alarm or celebration, but we remember what we did inexactly (or not at all). It was not under the direct control of our conscious mind.

The second category we will call "intentional." To assist with giving directions, we may point North. We may open our arms wide to make clear our amazement. We may push our hands and arms out and away from us several times to get someone to "stay away" or "go back." We may make descriptive gestures representing a sword fight or the movements of a snake. We gesture in a certain way with, usually, a certain goal in mind. Very often, the actor abandons this second category because it might "seem hammy" or "be too much." The intentional gesture is crucial to the actor. There is an element of control in the actor's work, an element of the bullfighter who strolls up and kisses the bull between the horns, and the intentional gesture manifests that.

Intuitive gestures tend to start from the thigh and drop immediately back where the impulse loses force. By so doing, the gestural vocabulary becomes predictable, always starting in the same place and returning there, often with the telltale sound of a thigh slap. Now, obviously, we are desirous of mixing these two categories of gestures as we act. The intuitive will take care of itself, but the intentional is a choice made by the actor or character. Let's do an exercise.

Exercise
A
What I want you to do is... *(Points at other character)* get away from me. I'm not talking about what happened today, I'm *(creates a circle in the air with both hands ending palms up at the waist)* talking about the whole thing. Do you hear what I'm saying...*(claps hands at the other character as is shooing a horse away)* move it out.

(Brings hands to a praying position)

Don't make me make any more of this.

Usage
This exercise lets the actor get a feel for the intentional gesture. *It insists on a specific physicality, not because it is "right" or "best" but to let the actor make a specific choice instead of leaving it all to the nervous system.* As with most of the exercises, it will be most helpful to let the actor do it two or three times before another actor does the exercise.

Coaching
You will notice that two of the gestures are illustrative. Creating a circle in the air illustrates the "whole thing," etc. The other two are more from the actor/character's personal experience or iconography. It must be made clear that we are not, God help us, simply asking for an illustrated performance. Physical illustration is a useful tool but can be easily overdone and then moves on to being unbearable.

Unbearable Example
I want you...

(points at other actor)

to pick up that suitcase...

(mimes the activity)

close the door...

(mimes the activity)

and...

(walks in place)

walk right out of here.

(Draws down an imaginary window shade).

End of story.

(Sound of audience running screaming from the theatre!)

USAGE

In the next exercise, we want the actor to use three intentional gestures. Each gesture is then held where it finishes (if you point, you hold the point) until the next intentional gesture begins from that position. The last such gesture is held, at its completion point, until the end of the speech. This is done to show that all gestures don't begin from thigh level, nor do they return there as the intuitive gesture does.

EXERCISE

I don't know, my first thought was that it was all over. I was falling. I'd lost my grip and I was in mid-air maybe two, three hundred feet above the river, and there was nothing, nothing I could do about it. The river and the rocks moved up toward me, instead of me moving toward them. It took an unbelievably long time. A new kind of time experienced in a new way. Then I hit the water. This is so weird, I thought, I'm alive.

Coaching

The intentional gesture is controlling. Tell the actor to use it confidently, to give it a beginning, a middle, and an end. If the character is not in control, they might use the intentional gesture to appear as if they are. Make sure that not all such gestures are illustrative. Some are more abstract as in pounding the table for emphasis, or extending the hands palm up to signify surrender. Remind the actor that they choose this gesture, they present it, they hold it, and then they let it go. It isn't just a blip in the nervous system. Remind the actor that the intentional gesture is rarer than the intuitive gesture. If it is overused, the work will, in fact, look stagy. Have them do the exercise more than once and change the nature of the intentional gestures they use.

Usage

In the next exercise, the actor should use only one intentional gesture (though as many intuitive gestures as her nervous system produces). The simple gesture should coincide with whatever moment the actor feels is the most important in the speech.

Exercise

A

Time up, okay? I can't take this anymore. I wasn't created to do your bidding. I'm not your upstairs maid. This is an equal deal or it's no deal. Do you get that? Let me try to simplify this for you. Don't tell me what to do. You can ask me but don't tell me. Now let's do this once more. What is it I can do for you?

Coaching

Ask them why the chosen movement is the most important in the speech. Unless the reasoning seems truly absurd, do not question it. Make sure the intentional gesture is done fully and confidently. If not, ask that the exercise be repeated. If the gesture chosen is illustrative, say that is excellent but ask that they do it one more time with the chosen gesture being more abstract. This gives them practice in both categories.

HELD GESTURE/CONTROLLED DROP

This is a quick follow-up to the work on intuitive and intentional gestures. It is a continuation of our thoughts about the intentional. Let's say for demonstration that the actor has spread his arms wide as he/she says:

A
You are driving me crazy!

At this point, many actors simply release the gesture, letting it fall back to their sides from whence it came. Rather than that, *A* keeps the gesture where it ended up (arms spread wide) and continues the line with the gesture still in place.

A *(cont'd)*
How many times are you going to say the same thing?

(Arms still wide)

Do you think I don't hear you, or that I'm stupid or preoccupied? What is going on in your tiny mind?

Now actor A *brings the arms back to his side in a controlled manner (he doesn't drop them like a dead weight). This is the controlled drop. Either while so doing, or afterward, he says:*

A
Okay, okay, I'm sorry. I'm a little cranked out.

This is obviously mixed in with our physicality and not done every time you gesture. It is simply another way of handling gesture and part of the mix.

Usage

We will now use the same shard of monologue and let the actors use it exactly as described. Keep an eye on the actor maintaining their concentration as they hold the gesture. The character isn't thinking of the gesture. They have actually forgotten about the gesture being held and are ferociously playing the objective. Also demand that the controlled drop is exactly that. Let's do an exercise where the actor chooses the gesture, the moment for the gesture, and the moment of the controlled drop.

Exercise

A
(Speaking to a listener)
So, Joey and Lisa… You know Joey and Lisa, they leave this party at… I don't know, late. And they're as usual, arguing about whether they should break up. Yada yada yada yada. And paying no attention they drive the Jag *under* an eighteen wheeler. Bam! Not hurt, okay, but trapped. Took firemen an hour and a quarter to free them, and they were still arguing as they pulled them out! Joey and Lisa.

Usage

The point of the exercise is to find the moment of a gesture, hold the gesture and keep talking. Then bring the gesture down in a controlled drop.

Coaching

Remind them this is not to be overused. Make sure the gesture is held for a sentence or two. Make sure it is brought down in a steady move to the actors' sides. The point is to break old habits, feel differently in your body, and open yourself to new physicality.

THREE GESTURES

The actor has a gestural vocabulary just as they have a spoken one. This implies that the actor currently has gestural limits as well, and those limits are cruel definers of their work onstage. As each character has a gestural vocabulary, the sense of character must be limited by what the actor's body is used to doing (gesture, of course, is full body). *How can we increase the actor's physical vocabulary?* Well, observation surely, but the next step after observation is practice. So, practice we will. There is another self-imposed limit on gesture, and I believe that to be the mistaken sense that gesture is: 1) embarrassing, 2) it interferes with our sense of honesty on stage, 3) the larger the gesture, the fiercer the psychology and want behind it must be. The student actor often wants to be good without being *noticed*. I know, I know, odd but true. We need to encourage the actor to go where they haven't been before and thus to realize no harm will befall them and good may ensue. I am suggesting that they open up the possibilities to better serve the character and situation when needed. Large is rare, yes, but often powerful. Eccentric we see almost every day in our passage through the world. Let's practice going a little farther than our current vocabulary.

USAGE

The instructor is going to demonstrate three gestures. For the first exercise, let me suggest them: 1) Some version of both hands, above head level. 2) Clap three times. 3) A wavelike motion done with the left hand going a good distance from left to right. Now in the following monologue, the actor must use these three but in any order they wish. Are other gestures included? As the actor wishes but these three are demanded. The trick as usual is to make them serve the psychology and circumstances of the speech.

EXERCISE

(There is a listener, B)

A
You know, there's a point where you have to get off my back. Yes, I am a little non-communicative. Yes, I am a little irritated. Yes, I'm on the Blackberry more than I should be. And yes, you have a right to tell me these things in that patronizing, fake-cheery, carefully calm voice. But I'm not listening anymore. Look in my eyes, the lights are off. Nobody home. End of story.

USAGE
The gestures could go anywhere. They could be used at three separate moments or laid end to end in one place. The point is to demand a scale of gesture young actors don't always commit to on their own.

COACHING
Some of the actors will size down the gestures to miniature versions of what has been requested. Don't let them get away with it. Others will do the gestures in an unrecognizable form. Ditto. Others will only remember two of the gestures. Request a re-do. The class usually finds the exercise fun and amusing. The variety found inside such a tight construct is a lesson all its own. The point is that gestural vocabulary is allowed. They should be exploring. What they've got now isn't enough. Now, keep the same monologue and give them three different gestures. (Touching the floor is always a good one. So is a kick. It doesn't all have to be the hands.) Finally, to close out this section, I ask them to take the original three gestures and use them in one of their auditions pieces. If

they haven't an audition piece, you can assign the following monologue.

A

I don't know Mom. I don't think I can actually apologize to him. I actually think he kind of got what he deserved and the fact that it happened in front of his so called friends, particularly Sal, well, if the truth be known, I get off on that. The fact that his car looks a little different now? Hey Mom, stuff happens. And by the way, do I smell meatloaf.

FINAL NOTE

This concept and exercise doesn't reach a single craft skill but opens the door on the pursuit of gestural variety and openness, so necessary to the complete actor. It doesn't deal specifically with the idea of each character having such a vocabulary, but hopefully it will plant the idea to be harvested later.

The Helicopter

This is for fun but, additionally, it can make for a memorable moment. Also, for entertainment value, I provide the actors with a mock contract to sign, agreeing to using "The Helicopter" once during their careers and to phone me when they do (five have phoned so far). I first saw the helicopter used by Julie Harris in Carson McCuller's *Member of the Wedding* (yes, I am over the hill). It was ecstatic and I have never forgotten it. And that is the nature of The Helicopter, celebration. A moment for the character when words won't express the joy of triumph. You know what it is by now. The actor spins in place, arms extended. Twice around is all right, but three times is best. Nice quick spins, please. An accompanying sound gets extra credit.

Exercise
    A
    Got dressed up. Really dressed up. Hired a limousine about two blocks long with a guy in a red chauffeur's suit. Filled it with, an exact count, six hundred roses. Iced champagne up front. Brought along my two nieces as flower girls. Walked into Bradley & Kaiser Accounting, sashayed up to her/his desk, played a tuba solo and asked her/him to marry me!

    (Does The Helicopter. The following line can be done during the spin or afterward.)

    (S)he — Said — YES!!

Coaching
    Don't accept less than three full rotations!

THE VERBAL

THE RUN-ON SENTENCE

This technique is used in our work on rhythm, but often the actor plain old forgets it's available to her. I have, more than once, had undergraduate actors of some experience say naively, "So it's alright not to stop at a period?" Yes, that's an undergraduate at the very beginning of a career, *but I've also sat through professional productions where respect for the period seems almost theological.* They must have been formed by eighth grade Mussolini-s of punctuation. I'll go out on a limb here (not really). Yes, there are many times you may run sentences together with no respect whatever for punctuation. I know, I know, not as often in Shakespeare. Why would we? Emotional momentum causes it. The quick mind embraces it. It creates a semantic structure that allows you to focus a speech in the way you want to. It creates rhythm, which freshens the ear. It's the way people talk. In these exercises, we're going to concentrate on running two sentences together because we'll talk about larger blocks in the work on rhythm that follows this.

EXERCISE
A
This is a prepared speech. *I would like to kiss you. I would actually like to kiss you several times, several times a day.* I know it's a little dweeb-like to ask for permission.

B
Wow. You are truly like out of the 19th century. *The problem is, I like you. I have literally no interest in anything but like.* I would, however, like it very much if you would take me to dinner.

Teaching The Actor Craft

Usage
Each actor should run the underlined sentences together.

Coaching
Make sure the run-on sentences are played with literally no pause in-between but that there is at least a half beat pause before and after the run-ons so that we can distinguish them. Here's another one.

Exercise

A
I *think that ankle is fractured. I don't think that's a sprain.* You can't make it down. You take it easy, I'll go for help.

B
Look, it'll be dark by the time you get help. It'll be three times as hard to find me in the dark. I can get down. Don't give me that look.

Coaching
Same rules as the previous exercise. Make the run-on sentences clear as distinct from the other sentence. This technique is usually immediately clear but let's do one more. Here the actor needs to choose the place and put three sentences together as a run-on. Two could probably be done with sentences of any length. Three would probably need sentences of shorter length. Oh, by the way, yes run-ons may exist in Shakespeare.

Exercise

A
Please, I don't mean to creep you out by being depressed. This happens to me. You just haven't had the good luck to see it before. This is me several times a year. You look literally stunned. This is still the me you know, it's just the part you haven't seen. Now you see it.

B
I'm not creeped out, okay? If this is you several times a year why haven't I seen it? What do you do, go off to the bathroom until you're cheerful? It's just a little disappointing that you haven't trusted me with who you are. Actually that does creep me out. What else don't I know?

USAGE
Each actor very clearly runs three sentences together. It can be at the top, the middle, or the end.

COACHING
It needs to be perfectly clear which three sentences compose the run. If it's not clear to you and the class, the exercise must be repeated. To finish this section, you might want to see the class target scene and ask that each actor put a two sentence and three sentence run together somewhere in the scene. If you don't choose to use the scene, you should certainly ask to see run-ons used in an audition piece they use. In general, run-ons are used to build less important sentences together a group. Or it may be a way to make a coherent single thought clearer through the run-on. In any case, the idea should be part of every actor's arsenal. This is important enough to the actors that you might have them give the idea a try in Hamlet's "to be or not to be" soliloquy, as an assistance to the speeches coherence.

ATTITUDE
Yes, I hear the line. What's the characters attitude to the line? This is at the center of the actor's work and seems an eminently sensible pursuit, but far too often the actor has not made the choice. The attitude toward the line defines the psychology, the thought process, and indeed the action or objective. Without an attitude toward the scene, the scene invariably deflates. The "attitude" toward the line is so much a product of given circumstances, backstory, objective, and psychology

that it really shouldn't be considered a "craft." What is a craft is the actor's ongoing determination to reveal the attitude.

Usage

We are simply going to deal with the need to have attitude toward the line often enough, and in a repetitive way, in the hope it will stick as a necessary part of the actor's arsenal. Here's an exercise.

Situation

A man or women needs to declare their love. They feel they have waited too long to do so, and now the object of their affection is planning to go to Europe for an extended stay. It is now or never. Dinner is over and the loved on is busily moving around and cleaning up.

Line
"Whoa, hold it, can I get you to sit down for three minutes."

Attitudes

Here are five attitudes that might occur in the situation.
1) Irritated because you can't get their attention.
2) Warm and affectionate because she is always doing.
3) Nervous because who knows what the answer will be
4) Clear and demanding because it's important.
5) Ironic because she doesn't sense what you think is obvious.

Usage

Now put one person onstage as the busy bee and let another actor sit watching them and then say the line. This will be repeated five times using each of the five example-attitudes. This is then repeated by each class member. Now each class member does it once more using a sixth attitude they themselves choose.

COACHING

Can each of the six attitudes be observed as different from the other five? Is there, in fact, an observable attitude? Do you believe them when they play the moment? Here's another exercise.

THE SITUATION

A person who has been out of work for eight months has had a job interview that seems extremely promising. On the way home, this person had several drinks. It is even possible they had a couple before the interview. You are the beloved sibling. They called and informed you he/she didn't get the job. Now have the class list five attitudes the actor might have toward the following line.
Line
"I took the call, you didn't get it."

USAGE

Using the five attitudes the class can agree on as possible in the situation, have each actor (with a second non-speaking actor) play the line all five ways with a ten second rest period between each of the five.

COACHING

When the scene or audition is being shown (worked on), simply respond at various times, "I can't tell what the attitude is, go back." When the actor cannot solve the problem at hand, the scene needs discussing until possible attitudes emerge for rehearsal testing. Remember the attitude reveals character, thought process, and objectives. It is the visible tip of the psychological iceberg. In any case, it must exist. It is important however to introduce the idea of "neutral" into the "attitude" work. The character uses neutral when:
1) They don't know.
2) They don't want to say.
3) They are restraining emotion.
4) They want to be "objective."
5) They are using "neutral" as a calming force.

Thus, "neutral" (unrevealing) is, in fact, an attitude, and one the actor will often find a use for. Let's close the section with an exercise in neutral.

Situation
Three siblings have returned home because of their mother's death. They are discussing the funeral and whether the body will be interred. The discussion has become an argument and the argument has become, well, heated. One sibling, you, has not stated an opinion. An opinion is demanded of you.

Line
I would personally prefer cremation but I think my real opinion is, Mom doesn't care.

Usage
The point is to achieve, as far as possible, a neutral presentation. The reason might fall under one or more of the categories I mentioned.

Coaching
"No, I don't believe that is neutral. It seems colored by_____." Some actors can achieve neutral easily, others struggle. Keep after the strugglers. When everyone has tried, have them do audition pieces attempting to find moments in them where neutral would be valuable. Neutral is particularly valuable to high energy actors who overuse emphasis. Tell them to just "say" the line, not "act it—simpler—less emphasis. Be boring." When they get it, it can be a game changer.

Spreading the Line

As actors, directors, and teachers, much of our work in delivering text is based on the idea that certain moments in the play, the scene, or the line are more important than other moments. The importance may be a matter of plot, a matter of character, a matter or clarity, a matter of emotion, but sometimes whole scenes lead up to it and sometimes it's choosing the key sentence (or every single word) in a single speech. *Taken together, these important moments explicate the theme, the story, the character, or the emotional through line.* Often, a developed technique is necessary in making these moments stand out. One simple way of doing this is to spread the line. It's simple, and it's underused. By that I mean, many actors don't know or ever use it. Please, I don't mean to use it over and over again. It's a definite garnish—once a play or twice a play would be enough. It's like a concentrate; don't ladle it on.

So, here it is. Let's take the line, "I'm not going to do it." You could spread the whole line as in: "I'm–not–going–to–do–it." Or you could spread parts of the line as in: "I'm–not–going to do it." You might, in an elaborate example, spread the first part of the line, put the second part together, and then spread the last part. You wouldn't spread three sentences in a row. That would not only confuse focus but also be precious and damned annoying. Here's an exercise with the line to be spread starred.

Exercise
   A
   Please, I'm asking you as a friend. As somebody who cares about you. I can't explain it, you just have to

go there on faith. Don't take that trip with him. I promise you, you'll regret it.

Usage

The starred line above is long enough that you could, albeit a bit awkwardly, spread the whole line or a little more easily spread part of it. Here are two more exercises for the actor to choose the line, he or she wishes to spread.

Exercise
   A
   Oh please. You've got to be kidding me. He told that when? This is like hilarious. This person loves me? We met twice. Maybe twenty minutes of conversation. No, don't set me up. Well, you fixed one thing for me, the day isn't boring.

Coaching

The actor must fully commit to spreading the line. The usual difficulty is that they'll half do it, i.e. not take the necessary time. Also, use the exercise as actor dramaturgy. What is the most important part of the speech? Why? What circumstances was the actor playing? How does spreading the line affect the actor emotionally? Is there another line in the exercise worth spreading? Try it. In any technique presented in the book, a technique probably won't penetrate unless they do multiple exercises. Let's do one more exercise with two actors onstage, with each of them spreading one line.

Exercise
   A
   This painting sucks.

   B
   Thanks, glad I showed it to you.

   A
   I never get to criticize, right?

B
You call that criticism?

A
Yeah, I do.

B
It sucks how?

A
Technically, color-wise, balance, the idea of it.

B
Tell me what you really think.

A
You deflect anything anybody says.

B
Because I want to keep working.

A
But you don't care if you get better?

B
Don't patronize me.

Usage

This is also a good exercise to examine overload of the idea. Try it with each actor spreading twice; is that too much? Each spreading three? When we hit "too much," ask the class why. Technique always works best when it isn't noticed. We must always remember that technique must be backed up emotionally.

Coaching

"Back that up" is a useful phrase in all the exercises; we want the meaning and the emotion in the foreground and the technique in the background. However, when an actor first starts using a technique, it will be badly handled. Let it pass until the third or fourth repetition. Then tell them the technique being used is too apparent and thus not believable. Then have them try it again. *In all technique study, it's key, at some point, to move from the exercises to something the actor has already done or is currently doing.* Have them spread a line in an audition piece they've been using for some time. How about a speech from a play they've done or even a play in rehearsal (careful though, we don't want to incommode or infuriate the present director)? I often insist that each technique taught be tried in their audition material. They can also try it (if their partners are present) in scenes concurrently being worked on.

Breaking Up the Line

Most of the time people don't speak in full, uninterrupted sentences. Many times the sentence is rife with inarticulate sound (um, for instance), pauses (for a host of reasons), and rhythmic change. For instance, we could say, "Hey man, good going, you just stepped on my glasses." Or it could be, "Hey man *(pause)*, you just *(pause)* stepped on *(um)* my glasses." The variety of ways to break up that line are endless. *(Very slowly)* "Hey—man—you—just *(very quickly)* stepped on my glasses." Do we do this in Shakespeare? Probably not. In Tom Stoppard? Not much because his sentences are often so complex that adding spoken complexity ruins the soup. This sort of futzing with the line is best when the line can be easily understood, as in, "I'm going down to the store. I'll pick up the celery." It's way less helpful in "Unthrifty loveliness, why dost thou spend upon thyself thy beauty's legacy." *It's used best of all on simple, relatively short lines that are emotionally loaded.* For instance, "I'm just telling you I'm not getting married." Why, realistically, do people break up the line? Well:
1. I realize I don't know what to say.
2. I'm looking for the perfect word.
3. My emotion stops me from continuing.
4. For emphasis.
5. I lose my train of thought.
6. An idea suddenly occurs to me.
7. I realize that once said there will be no going back.

So, it is thought process that breaks up the line (and circumstance, of course) and that thought process must be present! Try one…

A

(Speaking to a loved one you know is dying.)

Read this, it's funny as hell and it's short.

Or this one:

A

(Has just won the lottery)

I am going to buy you a Tudor mansion in the lake district.

COACHING

What was the mental process that made you break up the sentences as you did? Explain each element. It's a little too heady, but it's worthwhile. Careful that breaking up the line isn't labored. Did you break it up so much it became confusing? Here's a short duologue. Each person should break up one sentence.

EXERCISE

A

I don't think he saw it coming. I asked him for the money in front of his family. It was as if he'd been physically hit.

B

That is so incredibly mean. Why would you do it that way? The guy is plain old broke but it's not a criminal act.

USAGE

Do it again. Break up a different sentence. Which was better? Why? Another possibility is word repetition as in: "That is so (break.) So incredibly mean," or, "That is (break.)

That is so incredibly mean." Isn't that playwriting? Yes. But used judiciously you will seldom get caught at it. Let's try one more where you break up two lines.

EXERCISE

A
I want to know if there's going to be layoffs? I heard it from different people. People who are close to the top.

B
I would appreciate it if you would be a little more specific. These rumors, you know, they can damage the people who spread them.

COACHING

If the circumstances were that A was a line worker and B was a floor foreman, then choosing to bring this up is dangerous to A. That might imply, "I want to know if... *(thinking about whether he/she should go on)...* there's going to... *(last chance not to lay the cards on the table)...* be layoffs? In B's speech, there might be a slight pause before and after "damage" to emphasize the chance A is taking by bringing this up. To repeat, there is always mental process behind the breaking up of the line. Unless, of course, the character has simply forgotten what they were going to say. Let's do one last exercise in a slightly longer form. Break up two lines in the speech.

EXERCISE

A
I just cannot believe you would say a thing like that. Is that supposed to be funny, or bold or some weird cutting edge, or what? I mean dignity is an old fashioned word but get yourself some, okay? You are talking about somebody who practically saved your life. You know that. Are you on something? Let's just erase all that and start this over. Erased. Listen, did you hear about Mr. Borke?

Usage

The speech is a tad long to be learned in class in under ten minutes. This is one that might be best if learned overnight and started the next class.

Coaching

However the speech is structured by the actor, it is devised to be language shattered by emotion. This character is upset, confused, dismayed, and probably containing an anger that is threatening to spill over. It is emotion that breaks up the line here. It should be messy. This person isn't working with words; they are overwhelmed by a situation that words can't accurately describe or measure. Don't let the actors get away with any icy form or intellectual construct.

Framing the Line

This is another way to foreground a particular sentence or part of a sentence. The point, as always, is the contextual desire to make a point of some importance. Random use is the devil's handiwork. This is another technique that's fairly easy to explain and use. *You "frame" a line by taking a noticeable pause before and after it.* Internally, the actor can handle the frame in several ways. The pause before the line can be because the character is thinking of what to say, is afraid to say what he ultimately does, is using the pause to increase the line's significance, etc. The pause afterward is because the character is waiting for a response, because they don't know what to say next, because they are emotional, etc. The pauses used in framing must be internally justified. In this exercise, the frame is starred.

Exercise
It was flaming hot. It was like sun through a magnifying glass. Yes, I left the baby in the car. I went in to get water and there was a guy who had collapsed in there. I don't know why I stayed so long.

Usage
Because the framing is being used, the actor might try a slightly quicker pace in lines leading up to and following the frame. It increases the frame's sense of importance. Here are two exercises where the actor should choose where to place the frame.

Exercise

I think we should wait it out. They might come around or decide to increase the offer or circumstances could change, you know that. I don't think this is over, yet. I don't think we're seeing the bottom line. Do you? I don't want to run.

Exercise

There was a play, it just sucked is all. You ask why everything we touch turns to dust? Because we're optimists, Marco. We think because we're smart the world owes us a living. It doesn't work that way. The success is all in the preparation. We have to work harder at this.

Coaching

Are the framing pauses held long enough, and, more importantly, are they filled? If the actor is doing the framing but the pauses are lifeless, examine their thought process and the circumstance. Is the sentence chosen the right one to frame in the speech? Have them try another one. This exercise is perfect to clarify the acting fact that technique must be accompanied with a rich, functioning inner life. Empty pauses solve nothing, say nothing, and provide no assistance. You can also use a half frame if you want to weight a first or last line. Here's an exercise where each actor may choose where to frame, or half-frame, a line. One apiece would be fine.

Exercise

A

I know you don't give a damn but I'm glad to see you. Do you want to sit down? Yeah, same old chair, I had it recovered. You look like you just stepped into a time capsule.

B

And you look scared of what I think. How long did you leave Dad alone? When did you call 911? I'm sorry, sit down. You must be tired.

A
We went over this. More than once. Can we just try to be siblings? It's been like three years, for hell's sake. Can I have a hug?

B
I didn't come here for a reunion. I came to find out if Dad had to die. Frankly, I don't think he did. There are things I have to know for my peace of mind.

COACHING
To reiterate: give the class five minutes to learn the exercise. If they are still memorizing, give them eight. If the exercise is partnered, you could give another five to eight for them to rehearse together. Everybody can rehearse in the same room. Now let them perform the work more than once. Give quick/clean feedback. Now move on to another exercise. The point is to get everyone in class on their feet. They also benefit from watching others do the same exercise they're doing. You (the teacher) shouldn't be talking more than a minute or two at a time. The learning is experiential.

Throwing the Line Away

We being with the premise that not all the actor says is crucially important. That implies that we wish to make more of some lines and less of others. The question on the table is, "How do we go about making 'less.?'" The age-old practice of "throwing away" a line is seldom in the student actor's repertoire. Youth tends to throw acting energy at almost any problem. The idea of creating moments of unimportance seems counter-intuitive. Throwing away the line is usually done by using a relatively rapid delivery while leaving the line uninflected in a tone that is not particularly energized. Try saying the following line quickly: "Just take the dishes out of your room and leave them in the sink." Now retain the quickness and leave the sentence without particular inflection. Don't single out words or phrases for emphasis. Try it. *Finally, with quickness and lack of emphasis in place, add a slightly quieter than normal tone.* Good. You just threw a line away. The same thing could be done with multiple lines until you get to what you feel important.

Exercise

A

I don't know, maybe it was last week or the week before. Sally and I drove down, it took maybe four hours, completely uneventful, four lane highway most of the way, good weather, nice driving. (now emphasize the next line in a louder, crisper tone:) *When we get there he comes out with a pistol.*

Usage
You want to throw away the entire speech except for the last sentence. Lines thrown away are usually easily understood constructions that don't demand a lot of help from the actor. When thrown away, they must still be intelligible and audible. *It is simply clear that they are not the heart of the speech.* Now try this exercise of three sentences. The middle sentence is to be thrown away.

Exercise

A
The point is that you and Joan are going to get a college education. *Where, what school, what discipline is completely beside the point.* I don't give a damn what Dad says, that's what's going to happen.

Usage
Now, a duologue. Each actor should throw away two lines.

Exercise

A
You look hysterical. What is the deal with your hair?

B
As if my hair means diddlysquat to you? I won an office pool and the prize was an appointment with this famous stylist guy. It was an NBA finals pool, the Lakers, all that stuff.

A
I tell you what, I really wish I had a camera. It looks like you put your head in a cage and a lion sucked on your head. I came over for tweezers. I have this monstrous splinter.

B

Over in that drawer under the microwave. You know I get damned tired of you making fun of me. No, not that drawer. The one over to the left.

A

I'm supposed to pretend I don't notice you look like an idiot? Ow, this thing hurts. You planning to go bowling with me looking like that? No way.

Coaching

Simple enough. Is the line being thrown away less important than others judged more important? Is it clearly, no kidding, thrown away? If not, it should be reattempted. Less emphasis, quicker, softer. The actor's lack of concentrated focus helps. Look away from the other actor. Look at your hand. Look at the floor. Turn away. There's the sense on the thrown away line that the character is thinking of something more important than what she's saying. That their mind is elsewhere. One more exercise.

Exercise

A

Larry, I'm asking you as an honorable person to tell her what you told me. It's a fifteen-minute drive, a lousy quarter of an hour. She's trying to make up her mind and you can make it up for her. I don't know why I even have to talk to you about his.

Usage

Try throwing away one line. Then do it again throwing everything but one line away. This is a powerful tool and the actor needs to be expert.

Closing it Down

This is simple really, but useful. The scene may be seven minutes long. The play may be two hours. The point is, the character doesn't know that. There are many points in the play where the characters feel they are done, finished. They don't want to argue about it anymore, they don't want to discuss it, for them it's over. And then, of course, something is said, or felt, or information is given and it goes on. Look for the moments where the character "closes it down."

Let me give you an example. A man and a woman are on the edge of breaking up a long-term relationship. Things have been said and done; it's a moment of crisis and decision.

Exercise
Man
I don't think you see me anymore. You act like you don't know me. Right now… Right now I feel like I'm in the room with a stranger, a passerby. I'm alone here with you, and I mean alone.

Woman
Because I don't want to fight! You pick at me, you hassle me, you're not satisfied 'til we're yelling.

Man
I'm not yelling now. This is not a fight because I'm way, way past that. I am keeping the key; I'll come back for my stuff. See you.

Woman
I love you.

Man
Wow, you are something else.

USAGE

The point here is that when he says, "See you" he has to close down the scene. It's over. It's done. The plan is concluded. It's a curtain line. There will be no more dialogue. And then, of course, there is. Bringing to mind the old saw... "It ain't over 'til it's over." A play has many conclusions. Sometimes two or three in a scene.

COACHING

When this short exercise is played, demand of the actor that he bring the scene to a conclusion (a definite, unambiguous conclusion) with the line, "See you." If it doesn't seem definitively final, have the actor do it again. And again. Strangely enough, *actors have problems truly committing to mid-scene finality, perhaps because they know the scene goes on.* You often have to say, "No, *more* final... more definitely a finish." Then you have to say it again and do it again. Some actors will have to repeat the scene three, four or five times. Be firm and patient. Ask for repetition until you feel the actor has truly closed it down. Now the characters can be reversed so the actress can practice the exercise.

EXERCISE TWO

A
Come on, it'll be fun. You'll know everybody. You'll be back by midnight, you can study torts 'til your eyes fall out. A little relaxation for the belabored P.H.D.

B
Okay, okay, don't tempt me with fun and/or relaxation. Really. Please. You go. It will give me pleasure to know you're dancing like a crazed person. Go.

A
I need you to come with me.

B
No.

A
I could really use your company. Really. It would be a bad thing for me to be there alone.

B
And why is that?

A
Because I am dangerously bored.

B
Come here. Sit down.

USAGE

Same thing. Actor B must "close it down" with the line, "No."

COACHING

When an actor closes it down, it must be unambiguous. It is a signal given that there is to be no more. If you feel there is still some sliver of ambiguity, it must be done again. One of the great advantages of closing a moment down is the acting complexity of opening it up again. The transition from "No" to "Maybe" is rich with possibility. In each exercise, watch how the actor gets from closing it down to opening it back up. If you don't believe they have successfully made the transition, ask them to do it again. I would almost dare to say that repetition is the soul of art. When the actor has accomplished the goal, reverse the scene. One of the goals here is that the actor will scan the scene to see if an opportunity for this technique exists. Is "closing it down" at the chosen moment useful? The actor won't know 'til they try it. One more exercise then we'll move on.

Exercise

A
You look like you don't get it. Facts are facts. The guy was playing you. You can't trust him as far as you can throw him.

B
I lent him ten bucks. Big deal. Go easy, okay. This is not a matter for a criminologist. If I get played for ten bucks I will still wake up in the morning.

A
It's symptomatic, see, that's what you don't get. This is like boiling a frog to death by raising the temperature one degree an hour and the frog never knows it's dying.

B
Could we in a nice way agree we are maybe exaggerating here? Plus, I believe the frog knows when it's boiling. My thought is, we should go out and eat Italian.

A
You get vulnerable with this guy, you set a patterns, it will get a lot more painful than ten bucks. Don't be a fool here.

B
I'm not a fool.

A
Sorry, that was a little rough.

B
Italian. I'll buy the appetizers.

A
Case closed. Let's go.

COACHING

The close out is "I'm not a fool." However, other opportunities exist in the exercise actor B (or more accurately, character B) may feel he/she has had more than enough of the conversation and try to close it out after "Plus, I believe the frog knows when it's boiling." Also, character A could close after "Don't be a fool here" or a line earlier after "...it will get a lot more painful than ten bucks." Can an actor attempt to close more than once in a section or scene? Absolutely. Can both actors (or more) attempt to close in the scene? Absolutely. Obviously after attempting to close several times, the character will give up the tactic and further engage or leave. Closing can be assisted by gesture that lets the scene partner know "That's it!" Keep after the actor for the sense of finality. After finality, there is a transition to whatever comes next. While I seldom use class members as examples, I find that some people really get this idea and others struggle. If you have a class member who is expert, it isn't wrong to let that person demonstrate. In almost any craft exercise, some will be better than others. Repetition usually solves the problem (which is why all the techniques need more than one class day). If all fails, be satisfied with progress from the student and move on. *These are crafts some students cannot, at the moment, master. They'll retain the idea 'til they're ready.*

USAGE

The last exercise in this section is long enough that you may want to assign it overnight in terms of memorization.

The Cut Line

Over and over, the actor will confront the following problem…

A
Look, I just don't…

B
I don't want to talk about it.

Now, what to do? Well, both A and B have decisions to make as actors. Either A is cut off by B or there is a reason A stops. Actually, there could be myriad reasons. Allow me to list some:
1. A stops because he isn't sure what to say.
2. A stops because he knows what must be said but is unsure how to say it.
3. A stops because he has decided not to say it.
4. A stops because he is searching for just the right word.
5. A stops because he is afraid to say it.
6. You decide what six is.

B's choices are:
1. To jump in with his line right after the "t" in "don't". (We won't list the myriad reasons why he might but A off).
2. To let A's broken line hang in the air for time spans varying from one second to ten. Reasons he might do so are:
    a. He thinks A will complete the line.

b. He's enjoying A's confusion.
c. He's thinking his own thoughts.
d. He can't think of what to say either.
e. You decide what "e" is.

It is this combination of possibilities that makes the broken line fascinating. The broken line is all about thought process. However, let's start with the easiest. B is going to jump in and with the tightest of cuing, cut A's line. On all cut lines, the speaker goes on to finish the line until cut.

EXERCISE

A
Yeah, really glad… Well, moderately glad you came back.

B
A very full-hearted welcome.

A
The only problem is…

(The rest of this line would have been: "the only problem is I already rented to someone else.")

B
I don't want to hear the problem, not even a little bit.

COACHING

Remember, we're cutting the line, not letting it hang in the air. Working in pairs, each actor should learn both A and B's lines so each has a chance to cut. Because coming in on the "s" of "is demands a hair-trigger response, some of the actors will need several repetitions. Either they won't pick it up fast enough or they'll jump the word "is" and we won't hear it. This is truly a surgical technique. Let's try a duologue where both actors have an opportunity to cut.

Exercise
> A
> Jimmy/Ellen, are you alright?
>
> B
> I think so; man that was...
>
> A
> We saw the avalanche start and we...
>
> B
> My first thought was, "Okay, this is completely over. This is what dead looks like." I ran like...
>
> A
> You want some water? We have...
>
> B
> The sound was incredible.
>
> A
> You can't possible know how glad I am to see you.

Usage

These exercises demand extra repetition. I've found that just because it's done well once doesn't mean it's truly absorbed. Because the exercises are short, it's possible to do one more round of the entire class in ten minutes. In teaching craft, the student must put up with a touch of boredom. Let's move on to addressing the thought process necessary to leaving the cut line hanging. Let's go back to the original demonstration exercise.

> A
> Look, I just don't...
>
> B
> I don't want to talk about it.

Instruct the students to take a three beat pause after "Look, I just don't..." (a thousand one, a thousand two, a thousand three). *Now, the point becomes why does A take the pause and why does B let the pause exist?* I gave a few reasons at the beginning of the section on broken lines. The instructor could, if wished, give them examples. Probably a little back-story would assist.

BACK-STORY

A has been taking care of B's dog. The dog escaped and was grazed by a car. The dog survived but the vet bills are heavy. Or make up your own.

COACHING

The teacher's concentration is placed on the pause. Do both actors fill the three beats of silence in a satisfactory way? If the actor is having trouble and the pause seems pro-forma, you might detail an example of a thought process for them, as in:

A
Look, I just don't...

(The rest of the line is "...know how to make this right." A stops because any excuse seems lame. B holds because he thinks A may have an excusable reason, or he expects an apology. When neither is forthcoming, he speaks.)

Another solution is very like the work we did on physicalizing the transition. For instance, A, on having stopped the line, walks to a chair and sits with her head in her hands. Now B is at a loss, pauses, and then finally says,

B
I don't want to talk about it.

Obviously, filling pauses with an appropriate thought process based on the given circumstances and/or an appropriate back-story is both a talent and a craft. This tiny exercise can be used to make the actor aware of this. Don't let the actor off the hook too easily. They need to succeed at this. If they just cannot, return to the exercise the next class period for those who are having trouble. Sometimes, a little breather works miraculously. Let's do one final duologue.

A
Wow. I can't believe you slapped me. You…

B
I'm sorry. Look, there's stuff I don't like to be called. Why would you…

A
Because you always do this.

B
Call you on your…

A
Take the argument too far. You have no idea when…

B
And you have no idea when enough…

A
And you do? I think we need…

B
Don't even.

Usage

Each character has two unfinished lines. With one of them, the other character should cut the line (come in immediately when the cue word is complete). On the other, A and B should agree to a pause at the cut and work to fill it. Thus each character has one of each.

Coaching

By now, the technique of cutting the line should have been achieved. The teacher reinforces the idea that the person whose line is cut continues the line until cut (this is the only playwriting actors are allowed to do!). Thus:

> A
> Look, I just don't…
>
> *(A playwrights continuing with "…want you to think it was my fault.")*

Unless B has gone completely asleep at the switch, the line will be cut long before the end of the sentence. What should be carefully watched and responded to now are the moments where both actors let the broken line sit in silence. What is each actor playing during that time? When the pause seems empty or forced, the teacher may inquire what each actor is playing in the pause and then have them do it again. As this is the final exercise using this technique, a brief discussion of its elements should be encouraged.

The Greater Overlap

In a certain sense, it's disingenuous to include this in our craft work. Directors and playwrights (particularly playwrights) are mad about overlapping dialogue. Why they are so fascinated when it almost always ends up as indistinguishable muddle, I cannot tell you. Since, however, it is part of the playwright's bag of tricks and actors are going to have to cope with it, we best have a go.

Since two people are going to be speaking simultaneously, which will probably obscure sense and meaning, what is to be done? Sometimes what is desired theatrically is simply a cacophony, a Tower of Babel, meant to deliver a sense of disorder, chaos, and each speaker's disregard for the others. In this case, little craft is needed and the actor simply marshals his concentration and proceeds as if his or hers is the only important voice. If, however, the audience needs to hear one voice rather than the others, one will need to speak softly and the other louder.

Exercise

A	B
I heard him screaming. It echoed down the canyon walls. And then suddenly it stopped. The silence was devastating.	I kept calling. Somebody help me. Somebody help me. It felt like I went on forever. Then I knew there was no use and I stopped.

USAGE

The two actors involved in the exercise should try one loud (meant to be heard) and one soft (meant to be a tickle of sound underneath the other). Once the proper effect has been achieved, they should reverse the procedure so each has an opportunity to be the major voice.

COACHING

Need I say? The balance will have to be adjusted until, one hopes, sense can be made of the featured dialogue. Usually, the speaker in the minor key will have to work much more quietly than one would suspect and the major voice must articulate with great care, with the consonants given particular emphasis. Success is not easy to achieve. Now let's try something a little more sophisticated. In this exercise, both speak at the same level, but one or the other drops out at certain moments so an individual line may be heard.

EXERCISE

A	B
No, I won't.	Absolutely not. There is no way I'll let it happen.
(Drops out)	The guy is an abuser and this isn't the first time.
He can threaten, lash out, I won't take it any more. I need you to take care of it.	*(Drops out)*
He's going to be here in, I don't know, five minutes.	He's going to be here in, I don't know, five minutes. Please.
(Drops out)	I can handle it.
I can't handle it. Thank God you're here.	*(Drops out)*

USAGE

This score gets (hopefully) certain key lines in the clear and hopefully reclaims some sense from jumble.

COACHING

Short as the exercise is, it will take time to perfect. I would suggest the teacher work only with one or two pairs and let the rest of the class learn by watching because they won't run into this circumstance often. The actors might be reminded that often when simultaneous dialogue is demanded, no one knows quite how to tackle it and they may be able to contribute these solutions. The one loud, one soft technique can also sort meaning out of dual speaking. Let's do one more exercise.

EXERCISE

A
I don't care any more.

(Louder)
You know I loved you.

(Softer)
But it's hard even to remember. I'm going, you don't have to tell me.

(Louder)
You can keep the ring.

B
I want you to get out of the house.

(Softer)
I flat out don't love you.

(Louder)
It's hard to remember when I did. I don't want to think about this.

(Softer)
Beat it. Go on. Go.

COACHING

Once again, you'll have to assist in balancing the louder/softer. It's almost impossible for the participants to judge. This kind of work is not only about decibels, it's about clarity. To keep a sense of reality while concentrating on the sound and reversals is a second level of the problem. It's an example of the actor's dual mind, both inside and outside the role simultaneously. These are techniques that come in handy, but are hard to enjoy.

The Lesser Overlap

This won't take a lot of class time. This easy overlap only means that we start one line during the final three or four words of the cue line. Where I put the slash mark in the cue is where the overlap begins. As in…

A
He always treated her badly. Always. Not that it is / any of our business.

B
This is the ninth time you have told me this. Enough already.

Usage
Go quickly around the room (the class may remain sitting) and have them do this two line exercise. Then go back and reverse it so everyone has done the overlap.

Coaching
You might explain that this simple overlap is used when there is no crucial information at the end of the overlapped line. Further, the actor who wishes to try an overlap should ask permission of the other actor first. As in "cutting off the line," the actor who overlaps must break cleanly in. Let's do a slightly longer exercise. This one on our feet.

Exercise
A
It was completely hilarious because he was locked out in his underwear. Can you / imagine that happening to him?

B
So, let me get this straight, he was locked out with the dog? How late at night / did this happen?

A
Really late-really, really late. And the dog didn't' like him in his underwear, so he started barking / like some mad thing.

B
Are you talking about when he had that giant German Shepherd?

A
Exactly. That dog was frightening, / so anyway…

B
I saw that dog chase two missionaries into a McDonald's. / They were petrified.

A
But listen, how did he ever get back in the house?

B
He didn't. He and the dog slept on the lawn.

COACHING

So, use this kind of overlap either when the characters know each other well, or in forms or argument or great excitement. Do not use when what is overlapped (or indeed, the overlap itself) crucially needs to be heard either in terms of plot or character development. The overlap can also be done in terms of loud and soft so that the person with more important words can be heard. Here's a final exercise where each actor makes a choice where an overlap might go.

USAGE

Only one overlap per actor, please.

A
Anna will be coming by so don't leave before six. I'll call later.

B
Are you kidding me? I cleared my schedule to work. Anna talks like a marathoner runs. I can't take this.

A
I told her she can't stay. She's just dropping off the research.

B
Don't do this to me, I beg of you.

A
Don't be your anti-social self. Come on, make a little sacrifice for me.

B
It's a good thing I love you. Go! Depart!

COACHING

Did the actors select places for the overlap where key lines are not obscured? Were the overlaps clean? Tell the actors that the sue of such overlapping should not be overdone, a couple of times will be enough for the evening unless overlapping defines a relationship or a character. It is a useful tool for the actor used in moderation and brings sense of spontaneity when well placed.

LIFTING

Many actors have a downward spiral in terms of vocal energy. The lines or section starts well, but as the actors breath is depleted, or simply because vocal energy is a task, the energy begins to fade. This is not, of course, a problem with a single sentence, but often the second sentence begins at the depleted level of the first and then declines further. The third is then begun where the second ended and the necessary energy winds it's way into oblivion. This downward magnetism causes another problem. At a depleted level, the vocal energy levels off and is continued on that one musical note. Thus, the other problem is lack of vocal variety. Both these problems may be addressed by lifting. *When the actor's text moves from one idea to a new idea, the actor addresses the new idea with increased vocal energy;* or, let's not beat around the bush, plain old talks louder. Let me give you an example.

A
It's always the same thing, Mama, always the same old song. How much money am I making? And however much that is, it's not enough, never enough. You always think I'm better than my take-home pay.

(Now lift vocally)

I don't care about the money. Well, sure, I care about it, but I'm not the money, Mama. You have to recognize that I'm a living, breathing human not a C-note.

(Lifts)

In case you don't remember, I'm your son James, not legal tender!

Usage

We might as well use this as an exercise. The women in class can substitute their own name and gender. The interesting thing about vocal energy is that many of us assume we're talking quite loudly when we're not. *Make sure there is a definite increase in the vocal drive at the point you lift.* You should be aware of the increase and so should the listener.

Coaching

Some actors do the "lift" clearly and immediately; others may have to repeat the lift two or three times. You may turn to the class and ask if the lift was aurally obvious? Truly shy souls have problems with this exercise. Press them. This is part of the craft that is habitual with experienced actors. *There is a certain vocal energy necessary to the stage.* If the actor is without it, or lets it drain away, the dramatic stakes seem low and the text not worth our attention. The over-energetic actor needs to find places to drop the tone down, but this is not our current concern. Let's use the technique in a duologue.

Exercise

A

I am… I don't even know how to describe it, bone tired. Completely out of gas.

B

You don't sleep. You lie there infuriated because you're awake. Just looking at you, I'm getting tired.

A

(Lift)

Oh my Lord, you should have seen Page today. It was casual Friday so she came in her pajamas. They had rocket ships on them.

B
I beg of you, don't tell me one more Page story. I get that she's the queen of the inappropriate.

(Lifts)

Wait. I forgot to tell you a check came for you. Whoa. Where did I put it? Why am I mired in disorganization?

(Lifts)

You should go in your pajamas. You have great pajamas. Pajamas by Matisse.

A
Do I look wasted or just attractively pale?

(Lifts)

What am I doing, where's the check?

COACHING

People are either doing this or they aren't. Be stubborn. There is no reason this can't be accomplished. Let's do one more where the actor chooses where to lift.

EXERCISE

A
My father, my father, my father. Why can't I stop talking about him? He's in my head like a splinter. I need someone to tweeze him out. He's still driving me crazy and he's dead. One time my sister tried out for this school play and who knows why, she didn't get the part. He gives her a hug and says, "Don't worry. It's only because you're fat." ! My father, my father. Whatever he thought, he said. What can I tell you, the guy was a monster. Do we have any Diet Coke?

Usage

The actor must find at least two places to lift. Three at the outside. Very often, there are several lines, or even most of a scene, before it's necessary to lift. We are a bit limited because, if we extend the exercise, the actors won't be able to learn it in the fifteen minutes we devote (no more) to line study in class.

Coaching

The same technical needs as in the other exercises pertain. What may interest the teacher here is whether, textually, they chose an appropriate place to lift? The reason I suggest the actor do so when a new idea is broached is that it assists the transition and supports the actor's interest in the new idea. The "Lift" also has value in calling attention to the line lifted so if it isn't signaling a thought change it must be either psychologically or textually (or both) important. You might also want to give a short summation of working with the lift, or even, God forgive us, a quiz.

The Unwritten Interjection

*Warning label: Don't do this with the playwright in the room!

Are you allowed to attempt to speak during other peoples' lines? Well, I use it all the time in contemporary plays. I think you can too, if used judiciously. The way it works will not surprise you. Here's the deal. A's full line is:

A
No way you're getting away with this. Do you do this with everybody? Do you steal from your parents? You are an amoral jerk.

With unwritten interjections, it looks like this:

A
No way you're getting away with this. Do you do this with everybody?

B
What are you…

A
Do you steal from your parents?

B
Hey…

A
You are an amoral jerk.

USAGE
The person without the scripted line only starts an interjection at the punctuation, usually after a sentence concluding period. The interjection goes on (usually one to four words) until interrupted by the resumption of the scripted line. The person with the scripted line *does not* need to hold for the interjection. They play in whatever rhythm they want. The psychology is that the speaker does not wish to be interrupted and continues. It creates a nice dynamic between the two actors and sometimes solves pieces of questionable writing, (Yes, Virginia, inadequate, psychology denying writing does sometimes exist in plays.) when it's hard to understand why one character remains silent while the other talks on. There are courtesies involved here. *If, say, you are going to try an interruption one time in the play, you should just go ahead and do it. If anyone objects, stop doing it.* If you would like to try such interruptions more than once in someone's speech, you should ask if they would mind experimenting with it. The majority of actors and directors don't mind because it deepens the sense of reality. *Do not over use.*

EXERCISE
In this exercise, places where an interruption might occur have been starred. Please, only for the sake of the exercise, try your interruption at these points. What these interjections are is up to the actor. They shouldn't be so interesting that we'd rather listen to the interrupter.

A
See, I was right, we should have turned left at the light. Why do I listen to you? Now there's a divider. I wanted a GPS, but no, that's too expensive. Now I missed another street. What time is it?

USAGE
Only interrupt at the marked stars, please.

Coaching

How does the speaker handle the interruptions? They do provide acting opportunities. Does the interrupter get the interruption started on time? It should begin flush against the final consonant of the sentence. Does the speaker clearly cut the interjection? There needs to be a sense of "Shut up" in the way the speaker continues. It could be a mean "Shut up," or a humorous "Shut up," and an "I'm not listening 'Shut up,'" but there is an insistence of continuing. *As always, most of the problems that arise will be cured by simple repetition.* This is a quick duologue with each actor choosing how and when to interrupt the other. EXERCISE RULE: No more than two interjections for each actor.

Exercise

A

You read about the hit-and-run on Magnolia? It's so weird because it was a blue Honda supposedly. I mean we have a blue Honda. They said out-of-state plates. We have out-of-state plates. I mean obviously it wasn't us. It's just, you know, coincidence.

B

Okay, that's interestingly put. It has this sense about it. The sense of, "Well, it's not completely obvious it wasn't us." Or, more specifically, that it was possibly me. You could ask me. You could say, "Were you involved in the hit-and-run on Magnolia? Go ahead, be blunt.

Coaching

Are the interjections handled so the actor using them actually seems to have written apt things to say in the situation? *The person interjecting must be able to complete the sentence when asked by the instructor.* Is it a good place for the interjection? Is the interjection handled well by the speaker? Do the interjections increase the aura of reality or do it damage? You could also ask the pair doing the exercise to do it again and spontaneously put the interruptions in different places. *Remind the actors that the person interjecting must need to speak. They are driven by a personal urgency, otherwise they seem pro forma.* It wouldn't hurt to do one more. Place and content to be chosen by the actor. Frequency is also a matter of choice.

EXERCISE

A
I can't... Look, I loved Dad. Yes, there were incredible disagreements, yes we fought, yes there were times... The point is I loved him. But you know I don't believe in cremation. I do not agree to burn him up like garbage.

B
You think I like it? I'm with you, I want a place to visit, a place to come back to. I don't want him just, you know, scattered on the ranch. I don't want to do that but he personally wrote the request.

A
And he's gone. This is about us now. He isn't up there on a cloud skyping about what we're doing. We've got the plot. Let's just bury him.

B
This is the last thing he wanted. And let's not get into it about life after death. We're doing what he said and that's that.

COACHING

You might try asking for increased frequency of interruption just to see it's effect on the scene. There is, of course, a point where we are disturbing the playwright's intent and that is usually a judgment made by the director. We should leave this particular technique with the full knowledge that we won't be using it in classical texts. Also, that there is delicacy and taste involved, and we won't always be right but the technique will be a useful one in a career. We have permission, limited, but permission nevertheless.

FLAT

Sometimes the problem is a sort of continual tidal wave of emphasis. The actor seems unwilling to leave the line alone. Emphasis takes energy, and this combination can exhaust. Indeed, emphasis clarifies the line and signals what the character considers important, but when words and phrases are heavily emphasized line after line, the audience can lose track of where the verbal focus lies. This is where the flat reading comes in. *"Flat" in this sense means that the character believes the point will be made without... well... acting.* I remember my father turning to a young actor in a production of *Death of a Salesman* and instructing, "Just say it, it's in English." I'll often say to an actor in the heat of rehearsal, "Stop acting. Just talk." The question arises, are we talking about the same thing as throwing the line away? No, we are not. Throwing the line away implies it's a line of lesser value, that not much would be lost if you hadn't heard it (in throwing the line away, you still wish to be heard). Flattening the line means to do the work with minimal emphasis, almost as if the words are powerful enough to make the actor almost unnecessary. You might, back in the day, have called it underplaying, but that, in a sense, means giving strongly emotional moments in dramatic situations a quiet tone. Flattening is a way of cleansing the listener's aural palette. Flattening give us relief from continual acting energy while allowing the line to make its point. Let's say the final line of *Hedda Gabler*, spoken by her husband is translated as "My God, Hedda has shot herself." It could go a dozen ways but to name three:
    1. *My God,* Hedda has *shot* herself.
    2. My God, *Hedda* has *shot herself.*
    3. *My God, Hedda has shot herself.*

And on and on. Flattening the line would be a clear, simple reading of the line (could be slow, could be fast), without words or phrases particularly hit. As opposed to the examples above, it would look like this:
4. My God, Hedda has shot herself.

When used after sustained emphasis onstage, flattening's virtues are:
1. A relief from energized sound.
2. Creating focus through simplicity.
3. A protection against working too hard.
4. A way of creating vocal variety that sustains the listeners' interest.
5. A way of engaging an audience rather than spoon feeding it.

*Warning: Flattening only works in combination with emphasis in a speech or scene; it does not replace it!

Let's do a short exercise, to clarify:

EXERCISE

A
(A second student should be B who listens.)

She drives away everybody I'm interested in! She's like some deranged, monstrous force field that's supposed to protect me but just completely isolates me! Literally, she's the sister from Hell!

(Now flatten the next two sentences:)

I know she's not well. I know I exaggerate her, but the result is the same; I'm alone.

(Now with more energy and emphasis:)

I can't sit here reading Tolstoy and wading through

chocolate like a pig at a trough. Living like this is a dangerous imbalance.

Usage

The actor needs sufficient drive, emphasis, and vocal energy so that when he/she goes flat, it reads. After the flattened section, emphasis and vocal energy restore.

Coaching

Make clear that the actor is not throwing away the flattened line. She/he allows their importance, but lets the words themselves do the work without pushing them out. So, it's not:

1. I know she's *not* well! I *know* I *exaggerate* her, but the *result* is the same; *I'm alone.*

Or:

2. I *know she's not well.* I know I exaggerate her, but the result *is the same*; I'm alone.

It's:

3. I know she's not well. I know I exaggerate her, but the result is the same; I'm alone.

You can also tell the student that the line could be broken up many different ways as long as "flat" is maintained. An example would be:

1. I know she's... not well. I know I exaggerate her... but... the result is the same; I'm... alone.

(Or a hundred other ways to break it up).

It is almost a guarantee that the first time through the exercise some class members will think they are flattening the lines when they are not. As actors, this seems counterintuitive. Just continue to encourage them to stop acting and just *say*. Yes, some slight emphasis remains, but you should emphasize *slight*. Also, there needs to be enough emphasis and vocal energy before and after to make the "flat" line different. Now let's work on a short duologue in which the flat for each is underlined.

EXERCISE

A
Wait! Stop. Hold it! This is all verbal fireworks, okay? I'm not even vaguely following this. Is she pregnant or not?

B
She doesn't know, she claims she doesn't want to know which is completely nuts. Of course she wants to know. Anybody would want to know! *I tell you this much, I don't understand her. Never did.*

A
Whatever the deal, this is just the kind of thing to put her out of commission. She can't make decisions. You don't think this is that slimy, cocky biochemist guy do you? You want creepy, there's creepy. This is a mess.

USAGE
Remember that for the sake of the exercise, "flat" needs to be surrounded by work using emphasis.

COACHING
Flat is just simple, straightforward work where the speaker feels the sentiments expressed, even when they are very important in the narrative, make their point without embellishment. It's a matter of saying, not acting. When the above duologue is acted, you are requesting that the underline "saying" is a contrast to the work that surrounds it. You can say "simpler" even when the students are performing the exercise. "Relax. Don't push. Just say it," is the coach's litany.

Usage

The percentage of flat, or just "saying it," in a performance is, of course, textual, situational, and interpretive. The important thing in the class work is for the student to fully understand what "flat" is and be able to feel comfortable with it. We should do one more exercise where the character, not wanting to relive the situation spoken of, keeps emotion at bay by using flat. In this case, the entire speech is flat.

Exercise

A

(With a listener.)
The baby, I don't know how this happened, the baby was in the middle of the highway in a car seat tipped over on it's side, back to the traffic, cars going by at seventy, eighty... Trucks, vans, eighteen wheelers. And this woman, older, heavy, had pulled over... She saw what had happened. She got out of the car, she was yelling at the traffic and she made a run for the baby and this truck, some kind of government van, the guy had a yellow baseball cap, he hit her doing high numbers... it was like a water balloon exploding and then he went over the car seat, too. So that was my day. Could I have a glass of water?

Note: This speech is long enough that it should be assigned the night before for memorization.

Usage

Each student does the speech twice. Once completely in the "flat" or "saying it" vein, and then a second time with flat and a more emphatic approach being mixed.

Coaching

Remind the actors that when flattening the speech, it is the character's attempt to distance himself/herself from the emotions felt. It is not unemotional, it is contained. And yes, there is emphasis, but it is used delicately so the speech is like two shades of grey. Remind the actor also that, when it seems apt, the sentences can be broken up. The second time through (it would be best if this were the next class period), it is the actors' call as to which parts might be flattened. When performed in these circumstances, you might make sure a contrast exists. Emotion in this case is allowed and then contained and then allowed.

USAGE
 "Flattening" is the actors' palette cleanser. It allows simplicity and straightforwardness a place at the table. It protects from overacting and over-energizing. It is the firewall against "too much."

The Rhythm

Rhythm Blocks

How many scenes, yes even plays, do you see where the acting is done line by line, each line a moment, and each line rhythmically identical to the last? For those with insomnia, this should be truly sleep inducing. What follows is a basic rhythm exercise based on breaking dialogue into units of different length and employing the run-on sentence as a key element. It is structured to make clear to the actor how many interesting rhythmic possibilities are instantly available to them.

Exercise
A
I was the first one to get down to the beach. The guy was lying on the sand. It was real clear he was dead. No doubt about that. He was wearing a black raincoat. He looked like he'd been blown up like a balloon. I just stood there. Other people got there. I didn't move, I didn't speak, there was nothing in my head.

Usage
There are nine sentences in the exercise. By using run-on sentences, you are to divide the speech into three units of one to six sentences apiece. If the numbers you are given are 4–2–3, you put the first four sentences tightly together, then take a pause. Then you put the next two sentences together, then take a pause. Now put the final three sentences together. Make sure they in the two pauses the exercise requires you continue the internal process you feel the speech deserves.

Obviously, you can make up the three numbers yourself, but here are a few to start with:

1. 3–3–3
2. 1–5–3
3. 4–1–4
4. 5–2–2
5. 3–4–2
6. 2–1–6
7. 5–3–1

Each actor should do the exercise two or three times using number combinations given by the instructor. Next, the instructor should give the group a mix of 2, 3 and 4 number combinations. Finally, the actor should break up the speech as they see fit and perform it one more time. It will be immediately apparent in the exercise that the psychology and emotional content of the speech will change greatly as the actor varies the rhythmic content. Here are two more exercises to be used in the same way.

Exercises
    B
    Oh my god, it was hysterical. The guy broke in and released all the rats in the lab. Then he opened the door between the labs. We came in, there were rats in all the equipment. They were in the pockets of the lab coats, rats everywhere. Some of us laughed. One guy fainted. He turned us into the experiment.

    C
    Please, don't do this. Please don't leave me. All my feelings are like glass right now. All the glass has fault lines. Please. Do it next week. Do it tomorrow. I sincerely ask you not to do it today. Please don't leave me. Let me get you a cup of coffee.

Usage
    These exercises should be broken up by the actor, rather

than the actor being given combinations. It is, however, useful to have at least two pauses.

COACHING

Remind the actors to keep the units together. If three sentences make up the unit, keep the internal pauses to a bare, split-second minimum. Encourage the actor to make the pauses between the units clear to the listeners. For the sake of the exercise, a three beat pause is better than a one beat pause. Make sure the pauses are used. Insist on a believable thought process. Obviously, the actor needs to create some given circumstances around the speech. Either you or the other actors, or both, can talk about the result of using different structures for the speech. What is the impact? Remind them that one of the values of the exercise is to impress on all of us that we shouldn't freeze our experiments with rhythm too early in the rehearsal process. Keep futzing. Also, the actor receives greater value if she does each exercise using more than one rhythmic scheme. Can this technique be used directly in audition, rehearsal, and performance? Yes. Eventually, this work should become intuitive and not mechanical, but we have to start somewhere. Can this work be done with exchanged dialogue? Yes, as you will see in the next given technique.

ENCOURAGEMENT

Enjoy the actors' success with the exercise. Remind them that acting work without rhythms that develop and change loses its audience. New studies show that attention renews at the point of rhythmic change. The question will doubtless come up as to whether this technique can be used for classical texts such as Shakespeare. The answer is both yes and no. This particular kind of rhythmic work is keyed to sentences of short or medium length where the run-on sentence can work for you. That suits some Shakespeare prose, but less Shakespeare poetry. Other classics have to be taken on a speech-by-speech basis.

Shared Rhythm

The previous exercise examined the actor's use of rhythm within single speeches and longer monologues. Shared rhythm depends on actors working together to produce rhythmic change. The principles of the exercise are shared with our earlier work.

Exercise

A
So, you're saying you didn't take the ring?

B
You're not seriously accusing me?

A
I'm seriously saying it's no longer in the drawer.

B
I didn't even know there was a drawer.

A
The truth.

B
The truth is you have no business asking me.

A
And why is that?

B
Because you trust me.

A
Did.

B
Then I'm gone.

USAGE
This is a ten line sequence. Break it up into three units, for instance: Three sentences, then five sentences, then two sentences. We will begin with the actors accepting imposed structures such as the one above, and then proceed to the actors creating their own rhythmic structure. As in our work with the single speech, we will make sure the pauses between units are substantial enough to read. Here is a second exercise for the purpose of practice.

EXERCISE

A
You think we should put the dog down?

B
I didn't say that.

A
And you didn't say not to.

B
I'm saying the time's coming.

A
Can we table this, okay?

B
You mean like last week?

A
I would like to spend a night off the death watch.

B
The dog can't do this herself.

A
Enough.

B
Fine.

A
Good.

USAGE

This one is long enough (11) that you could break it down into four units. Why don't you start with 2–3–1–5 and 1–4–3–3. Now make up your own. You can also do three unit work with the above. Let's try one more exercise.

EXERCISE

A
So you saw him with her or you didn't see him?

B
Maybe.

A
If it was maybe, why did you mention it?

B
Because I would feel dirt guilty if it was him and I let it pass.

A
But now the idea's in my head and I don't want it there if it wasn't him.

B
Just use it as a reference, keep it in the bank, you

might need it later.

A
God you are irritating!

B
If it was him, would you want to know.

A
Let's go to a movie.

B
You didn't answer.

A
No.

USAGE
Try working in larger units that time. It's eleven. Try 5–1–5 or 7–4 or 3–8. When increased pace is asked of you, that's one way to provide it without the same rhythm extending for too long. The idea behind all this is very much the same as it is in jazz. Establish a rhythm, break the rhythm, riff on the rhythm.

COACHING
Insist that the actors cue tightly so that the units cohere. *As in all acting, they need to listen to each other, pursue an action and vary the tactics.* Give each pair an extra five minutes to discuss (with these exercises, we must use the word "invent") the circumstances. As with every exercise, repetition promotes learning. You will find that actors immediately see the value of the exercise. They will ask how to get another actor to work in units in a production situation. The answer is to build positive relationships with those you're working with so you can suggest putting four lines together and see if both of you like it. At the very least, you can always put two lines together by picking up a cue. The real value here is to get the idea of rhythm into the actors'

canon. We will talk psychology all day, but often that work alone won't provide sufficient rhythmic content to keep the audience intent rather than lulled.

THE QUICK PART

Two things: Every scene needs a quick part. Every large speech needs a quick part. One thing: it shouldn't *all* be a quick part. Another thing, I'm talking about quicker than you think. *Maybe I should have said a really quick part.* Now, let's talk, about duration for a minute (and yes, it's all situational). In a speech of five sentences, you may want a single quick part. In a speech of ten sentences let's say three. In a scene, we might want one quick part of three or four lines. Impossible to really say. It obviously depends on the narrative, situation and psychology involved. However… the very nature of rehearsal often mitigates against the quick part. When we work to make every moment important and wonderful, the rhythm tends to end up as pretentiously methodical. Oh, please no. Anyway, let's play around with the really quick part.

EXERCISE
    A
    Good question. I don't know. I'm just up. An inexplicable natural high from who knows where. It just came to me actually, just suddenly felt incredibly good.

   (Now here comes the fast part:)

   Hell, I couldn't tell you, I don't even want to know and frankly you wouldn't care and I don't care if you care but I just feel great.

   (Now relax out of it.)

   So, if you would do me the honor getting out of this dump into some cold fresh air, I'd appreciate it.

Usage

It is basically a section where you can flat out rattle it off and we can still decipher the meaning. Now do it again quicker. To make the quick part really work, it's framed with more relaxed work on both sides. When I'm teaching, I often find the quick part is as foreign as Mars to many metabolisms and even odder (and sometimes amusingly so) a lot of young actors have no "rate sensor." *They actually think they're going quickly when in fact they are going slowly.* Odd. Let me say once more that playing a leading role at the same rate in the same rhythm for two excruciating hours is God's wrath visited on the paying customers. Now let's work on an exercise where the actor selects the quick part of the speech.

Exercise

Whoa. Hold it. You think I'm out of line here, that I contravene the opaque courtesy you assume is necessary to social function? Eat raw garbage, okay? I cannot tell you how sick I am of all this civilized muck you and I call a relationship and repeat endlessly as if something was actually going on between us, which, by the way, it isn't. Let me repeat, I don't like the way you treat me. I'm not your maid-of-all-work. Got it? Oh look, you're offended.

Coaching

Simply put, can you really, truly, tell the quick part from the other parts? Often, you can't and you can't leave that actor's work on the exercise until you can. *Usually, the quick part shouldn't be the most important part for obvious reasons.* Sometimes, though not always, we need an obvious transition coming out of the quick part. Or, to be blunt, a short pause. It's very cool if the actor can slow down without one, but that's advanced work. If the actor is having real trouble with the exercise, extract the two sentences and have the actor do only those until you are satisfied with the rate.

Now let's have two actors share the quick part (italicized).

Exercise
> A
> You said I was boring.
>
> B
> No, Kate told you I said that.
>
> A
> She was there, she heard you.
>
> B
> Kate, if you remember, hates me.
>
> A
> *That is so wrong*
>
> B
> *You completely know that.*
>
> A
> *You are such a creep*
>
> B
> The point is you're not.
>
> A
> Cross you black heart?
>
> B
> Read my lips, you are not boring.

Usage
> Really the same situation as the single actor use. Can you truly tell? Now, let the actors choose the section.

Exercise
> A
> Listen up. I really like you.

B
What is that supposed to mean?

A
Well, I was hoping it was a compliment.

B
Or maybe it's just kind of creepy.

A
That you're liked?

B
That you feel the need to say it.

A
It's worse because it's spoken?

B
Are those new shoes?

B
They are. Let's have a long talk about it.

COACHING
I'm sure you already get the point here. The question will come up as to whether, given the exercise, the quick part can be the opening or closing? It can. I only stick it in the middle so the actors can practice getting in and out of it.

THE SLOW PART

Having already done the quick part exercises, it won't be too hard to understand what we're up to now. However, it wouldn't be amiss to talk a little bit about slow generally. *I notice a lot of actors are talking faster than they can think and the result is often shallow, callow, and thin.* This is often the result of a personal addiction, or a directorial request, for "pace." Pace is often someone's Rx for the fear we're boring, or the text is boring, or the narrative is boring. *The problem that results is that boring isn't less boring when played faster*, and that which might be essentially interesting is made boring by going by us too quickly for us to sort out the interest. Now, faster" can help when what is said and felt is really quite simple and thus easily assimilable, but it's the aspirin of acting and directing, the nostrum given for all theatrical illnesses. I'm all for the actor fully understanding that it's valuable to put back some "slow." The following should be tattooed on some visually accessible part of our body: *There is no slow without quick, and there is no quick without slow.* I've spoken already about the fact that many actors seem totally unaware of the rate at which they are playing. I say, "Slower. No, slower than that. Slower still." By the third exhortation, they sometimes find the will and confidence to actually reduce their rate. Take the phrase, "I don't want to do that." It can be played in one gulp if absolute certainty rules the moment, but if there is any ambivalence, any confusion, any sense of insecurity, you will probably have to slow down to allow those things into the line. *Plus speed without variety tends to flatten the text* and sometimes makes it impossible to follow emotionally and intellectually. So let's look for the quick part and the slow part in an exercise or two.

Exercise
(The quick part is underlined, the slow part is italicized.)

A
<u>I'll take another cup of coffee if you don't mind and that's with much milk, no sugar, and I'd be pleased to get some honey if you have it.</u> *I would really like it if you'd take me back, because I'm changed and I'm ready to do this now.*

Coaching
Now tell the actor to do the slow part slower. Now ask them to do it even slower. See the value? The slow part, if we're working on prose, can have pauses in the middle. In the next, use a quick part, a normal part, and a slow part.

Exercise
A
Really, I thought you were crazy, what else could I think? I had never seen someone yelling at the conductor at the end of a concert. You were completely outraged about this tempo and that tempo and how the whatsits came in earlier than the other whatsits, it was pretty sexy actually. I love what makes you different, okay, and I'm getting the idea you don't recognize that. I do. It's shocking sometimes, how much the difference means to me.

Coaching
Don't argue about the actor's choices concerning slow, medium, fast immediately. Concentrate on whether the slow, medium, and fast are distinguishable from each other. After that's clear, you can discuss whether the tempi actually reveal the text. In this case, keep it in mind that it's the slow we're concentrating on.

Usage

The next exercise uses two actors and each should look for the moments where slow would reveal the text in an interesting way. But the rhythm needs to be mixed.

A
The point is, it was a four way stop, dude. You followed the guy ahead of you right through the intersection and when the guy on your left lays on his horn you go into this really creepy road rage. What's with that?

B
You are like addicted to criticizing me, really. It happens when I eat, it happens when I make the bed, it happens when I drive. Pardon the repetition, but what's with that?

A
We used to be friends. I don't criticize my fiends. Does that clear it up?

B
Yeah, okay, whatever. The guy on the left was an idiot by the way. He'd been sitting there forever. Why don't you go find some friends not to criticize?

Coaching

Ask the actors why they chose the slow part they did, what in their mental process seemed to demand it at that point? Slow is used for special emphasis. Slow is a product of the need to choose words carefully. Slow often signals confusion or mixed feelings. Slow means we're not sure we're on the right track. Slow means we really want the line to land, to have it truly penetrate the other actor. What was this slow? You might ask them to revise the work by finding a new place for slow? *Practicing technique always benefits from repetitions.*

THE PAUSE

Here we are in deep waters because, though seldom addressed in acting theory, the pause is often thought to be the province of emotion and spontaneous thought process and, as such, a bit of a sacred cow, not to be talked about as technique. If those who feel this way taught acting, they would realize that *actor fear and actor nerves coupled with directors who know no better than to pursue pace at the expense of detail often make silence an endangered species.* Let's conjure a bit on the pause. What causes it to appear in the midst of speech?

1. Can't think of what to say next.
2. Too emotional to speak.
3. Waiting for the other to speak.
4. Thinking.
5. Can't find the word.
6. Embarrassed.
7. Wishes to end the conversation.
8. Is taking something in visually.
9. Suppressing pain.
10. Doesn't want to say the wrong thing.

There are more, I'm sure, but they don't immediately come to mind. Mixed with these are a list of actors' reasons:

1. Taking the edge off the pace.
2. Taking the focus.
3. Making sure the rhythm in the scene varies.
4. Setting up an important line.

5. Framing a line (see table of contents).
6. Allowing an emotion room in the scene.
7. Rhythmic.
8. Allowing yourself to be seen. (In a certain sense, we don't see and hear at the same time. A pause often works on an audience the same way a close-up works in film.)
9. Creating dramatic tension.

There are more, I'm sure. The pause cannot simply be a product of interior life in the theatre because the pause giveth and it taketh away. Used at the wrong length, in the wrong place in the text, the energy in a scene departs like dishwater down a drain. Inexperienced actors use the pause too liberally and the flow of information passes more slowly than the audience needs to understand the text, follow the narrative, or retain interest in the character. This said, we have already dealt with the pause as an instrument of rhythm elsewhere in this book. Let's work first on "buying" the pause. The pause is easily taken off a build.

EXERCISE
A
I won't.

B
(Louder.)
You will.

A
(Still louder.)
And I say I won't!

B
(Loudest of all.)
And I'm telling you, you will!
(Pause. Three beats.)

A
(Quietly after the pause.)
You do what you want.

Usage

The build increases in volume with each line and peaks. The top of the build is good and loud, but not full out shouting. The pause taken is substantial, but not endless. The next line is spoken at about the vocal level of the first line in the build.

Coaching

The pause works where we've placed it because it surprises by breaking the rhythm and the ear has grown tired of the noise. Remind the actor that, regardless of any technique, the pause is always filled with a thought process suitable to the given circumstances. We are talking about placement, but we are assuming a workable psychology. The instructor (it never ends) will need to remind the class what three beats is. At least a third of the group will short the pause. Now the pause can also be "bought" by speed, not volume. In the next exercise, the teacher must insist on a substantially quick rhythm. Quick and light before the pause.

Exercise

A
So he bought the damn thing and paid four hundred for it.

B
I can't believe he could be such an idiot.

A
And then he forgot it at the store.

B
Incredibly weird. Was he doing drugs?

A
And then he forgot he forgot and paid for it twice.

(Pause.)

B
Okay, this is a joke, right?

COACHING
This only works if the first five lines go rat-a-tat-tat. With young actors, their idea of quick usually isn't quick enough. It is the instructor's call as to whether the pace has "bought" the pause. It's also a good time to talk to the class about how a strong emotional situation or moment also "buys" the pause. Also a moment of suspense "buys" the pause. The emotional situation obviously can't be replicated in the "exercise" format, but we can take a shot at suspense.

EXERCISE
A
What's in the box?

B
A little surprise. For your birthday.

A
You remembered my birthday?

B
Absolutely. Hey, I know you love animals.

A
What, a kitten?

B
No.

A
Not a dog, I'm away too much.

B
Definitely not a dog.

A
What, tell me?

(Pause)

B
An East Indian Hooded Cobra.

USAGE

Actors should learn lines for both characters so it can be done one way and then reversed.

COACHING

In this exercise, we should look at how long a pause will hold in a given situation with particular actors. With each pair, they should first use a three beat pause, then repeat with a five, then repeat with a seven. After each time through, the class should vote whether the pause "held." *The lesson learned is that a pause will hold at one length and drain the scene at another.* One actor can make seven work, another will have trouble at five. It can be asked why five didn't work for Anthony. Usually the answer lies in either the actor's though process and physicality during the pause, or in the way the two actors set up the pause. If one set up works and another doesn't, why? Obviously, no major pause should be taken prior to the pause we're working on. Let's do one last exercise to study the pause and it's frequency.

A
You lied to me. Now you're lying to me again.

B
Okay, I lied.

A
You think that doesn't matter? You think there's no damage done?

B
It's funny about you and the truth. You get it, you hate it, you don't act on it, then you ask for more.

A
You're all talk and no ethics, that's what I know now. What you say is all strategic, you squirm like a snake. The point here is no matter how we take the truth, we need it. I need it. Let's talk number — how many times have you stolen stuff from me?

B
Stuff you don't need. Stuff you never use. Stuff you probably don't even know you have. Can I tell you something, you live an abstract life and it screws you up. If you stuff something in the back of the closet and forget about it and I take it and sell it, what's your problem? It helps me and it doesn't hurt you.

A
I'll make this simple for you. Get out.

B
You always make it simple. It would be funny if it wasn't so sad.

(Actor B leaves.)

USAGE

This could be learned in fifteen to twenty minutes, or they could be sent home with it for the next class. This is an exercise not only in placement but in how many pauses a given scene or section might bear. Because, in truth, such things are deeply situational and circumstantial, we can only interest the actors in such problems without providing solutions. We want the actors to understand that the pause is not only a psychological matter but a strategic one. This is not a road map but an important understanding. It also gives the actors a chance to consider the internal pauses in her own speeches. I would start the first round by telling the actors each must use no more than two pauses of three beats or more. The next round, have each actor use three pauses of that length. Finally, last round where each actor uses five pauses. The point is to discuss placement, frequency, and the effect on the scene. This is probably going to take two classes or more.

Coaching

There could be a lot to talk about. It might even be worthwhile to start by playing the exercise basically without pauses and then begin adding silence as detailed in the usage above. That way the students can really see what silence adds, as well as the basics of how to use it. The points to examine are clear. Is the pause apt, does it deepen the moment? Are we taking too many? Are they too short or too long? Are they draining the energy or helping our sense of situation and character? The teacher's relationship to all this will be as individual as a fingerprint. It should be titled "Introduction to a pause."

Cue Pick Up

It might seem foolish to include this because in the most forlorn, least experienced community theatre group in the bleakest swamp in a town of one hundred doing, well let's say, Arsenic and Old Lace, and the director, a long haul trucker, involved in his first play, his face brightened with frustration, is yelling (at the very moment), "Pick up the goddamn cues!" It's the one thing about acting everybody, I mean everybody, knows. But we don't. Pick them up I mean. And because we don't, our small boat of creativity is swamped with meaningless pauses under whose weight we sink. And, as a concomitant, meaningful pauses don't exist.

That, we will speak more of anon. Let us practice this most humble of crafts.

> A
> Hey.
>
> B
> Hey.
>
> A
> Long time no see.
>
> B
> Longer than that.
>
> A
> You're still in Chicago.
>
> B
> Six years now.
>
> A
> Still with Jim/Sue?
>
> B
> That sank slowly in the west.
>
> A
> Sorry.
>
> B
> He/She died.
>
> A
> Died?
>
> B
> I killed her.

A
You killed her?

B
Joking.

A
Really?

B
Maybe.

Usage

To pick up a cue means simply that the sound of the line before has not vanished before the new line begins. If there is a silence, it is so infinitesimal as to be not worth speaking of. As the sound of the final "R" in "You killed her?" is heard, you say "Joking." Any reaction you have to the line in front of yours is played on (during) your line. Also, it doesn't take an excess of energy to pick up the line. It can be a soft or loud as you like, but it comes directly off the "R."

Coaching

As is many another acting craft, people think they are picking up cues when they are not. Make sure they do in the above exercise. Repetition will be necessary. Each person should *completely* succeed in the above exercise twice in a row before moving on. Now go back and allow one pause. Only one. The two actors can flip a coin for it. Now do the exercise a third time with each actor having a pause. They will now see how picking up the majority of cues give powerful focus to the rare pause. Finally have them do the sequence with a pause after each line and gage the effect (this can also be done on the first attempt at the scene). Project such an approach to two hours traffic on the stage and inquire the disaster. Nobody can say exactly what percentage of cues should be picked up, but it certainly never falls below 50% and often runs much higher. Have them do a final exercise.

A
I don't know, not really. He's said he's leaving a dozen times.

B
A dozen is the low end, but he's not easy to replace.

A
He's bluffing. Call his bluff to his face.

B
And if he goes?

A
He goes.

B
And when he goes we do what?

A
We pick up after him. We carry a heavier load.

B
I'm at the end. I can't, I won't do more.

A
Call his bluff. Get him in here.

B
Now?

A
Now.

Usage

Same drill, pick up all cues. But when you speak two sentences, you may take the interior pause. As in, "We pick up after him. *Pause*. We carry heavier load. The point is often that the pauses needn't occur at the line but it can be found in the middle. These "middle" pauses tended to be accepted as ""thought process," while those taken at the end can hang up the other actor.

Coaching

All final cues must be picked up. When they aren't, stop immediately and go back to the start. The whole point here is to have only interior pauses. Ask that the interior pauses be solid, two to four beats (a thousand one, a thousand two). And that's all there is to it. An introduction to the interior pause. Make each student do the exercise twice.

Beats as Rhythm

We talk about beats far more often than we actually make them part of the acting process. The easiest way to think of the beat is as a conversational unit. We talk about the Toyota. Beat one. We talk about the dissolving the marriage. Beat two. We talk about ordering pizza. Beat three. Yes, we can think more complexly about the beat changing when the action changes, but frankly that often makes the beats too long to be of any rhythmic assistance. What we're after here is not only rhythm but creating opportunities to act off the line, or, to be more clear, in the pause between two beats.

Exercise

A
Get the dog off the couch.

B
You do it, it's your dog.

(It's the end of the beat, take a pause.)

A
Why is it I'm always telling you what to do.

B
Because it makes you powerful. I makes you think better of yourself.

A
Very philosophical.
(End of beat. Take a pause.)
I think I have to move out.

B
We can't afford separate places.

A
I don't think there's a choice.

(End of beat.)

B
Dog's still on the couch.

COACHING
　Make sure a pause that reads is taken after each beat. It fulfills the exercise if each of the three pauses are of different links as in a two beat pause, a three beat pause, a five beat pause. Obviously these pauses shouldn't simply lie there like a deceased muskrat; they need to be filled with thought process. As with all the exercises in this book, it is best if each actor does the exercise twice.

USAGE
　These transitional moments at the point of subject change also prevent pace from overwhelming the acting. Runaway pace, like a runaway carriage, is likely to harm innocent bystanders. The filled pause provides a firebreak that out-of-control pace is less likely to jump. Let's try another exercise with the actors deciding on the beat change.

EXERCISE
A
Listen, I tried to call you, maybe it wasn't right on the hour, but I called.

B
And you are the innocent victim of technological misfortune?

A
No, you are the victim of never checking your messages.

B
Look, it doesn't matter that you didn't show. We had a great time, you weren't necessary.

A
Well, that's snide.

B
No, it's factual.

A
I would like the keys to the car back.

B
And you got here by what, helicopter?

A
I'm not going to miss your poison tongue.

B
I'll miss the way it used to be.

USAGE

Hopefully the actors rehearse and talk about the exercise only with their partner. It would be perfectly alright if every pair in the class found identical beats as long as they found them separately. The beat, like most acting, is a matter of personal (though hopefully informed) choice. In this as an other exercises using pairs, they can be changed at will for a second time through. It keeps the actors fresh and builds ensemble if there is time for discussion. It is helpful for everyone to hear why this or that actor put the beat in a certain place. It is not helpful to argue about it. A sample class might look like this: 10 minutes to learn the scene and assign pairs.

All pairs present the exercise. The acting coach discusses the results. All pairs present again. Each day, someone should be chosen to be on the book except when they present. The exercise could be continued in the next class if not everyone has presented twice. For the next exercise, the pair should be reformed so everyone works with someone new.

COACHING

If the coach decides to work in front of the class on a single pair, it should be to demonstrate principles rather than simply to "fix" the work. When work is finished on a certain section, such as "beats," I find it worthwhile to take 5 to 10 minutes to ask the class, "What can we take away from this exercise?"

The Build

A simple technique basically used by two actors but also a possibility for one actor inside a speech of some length. Let's use a four line exchange as an example.

A
I'm leaving

B
(Slightly louder.)
You're not leaving.

A
(Louder than the second line.)
Get away from the door.

B
(Loudest of all.)
No way!

What could be simpler than that? A progression of lines, usually between three and six in number, with each line louder than the one proceeding it, with the final line "capping" or "topping" the others and providing a final explanation point. *The build is usually found in moments of contention, excitement, fear, or celebration.* The build creates a focused energy between the actors that spills over into the audience.

Let's try one.

Exercise

> A
> I want you to give me back the watch.
>
> B
> Maybe in your dreams, fool.
>
> A
> And I want it now.
>
> B
> And you'll get it never!

Coaching

Oddly enough, there are many actors who have, at first, problems with the gradations of the build and who simply don't get louder on each line. Odder still, they firmly believe they are doing it when they are not. It is best to do the first exercise several times with rotating partners so you can observe who is actually building and whose ear is not yet attuned.

Exercise

> A
> I can't believe this, we hit it.
>
> B
> Two and half million dollars.
>
> A
> We hit the lottery.
>
> B
> Bingo!
>
> A
> What do we do about the other people in the office?

Usage
You will notice a fifth line has been added to the exercise. This is to show that another value of the build is to "buy" a pause (if wanted) after the build is capped. The first four lines are the build, then a pause. Then the fifth line more quietly. Let's try it.

Coaching
Once again, make sure it is a build, i.e. steadily louder. Then see what pause seems right before the final line. The final line is said at a level of the first line of the build or even below it. Have the actors experiment with the build, pause, and final line by doing the exercise a second or third time. Tell the actors that this provides a good example of how to "buy" a pause.

Exercise
Now we'll let the actors design and execute a build in a duologue. Remind them that we're looking for a sequence three to six lines in length.

A
Can you believe that he actually bought it? He thinks we knew him in third grade.

B
I can't believe you actually said that.

A
Loosen up, okay? At least it was funny.

B
I don't think it was funny, I think it was cruel.

A
How could it be cruel to meet some old schoolmates?

B
How about because it's a lie?

A
It turned a boring party into something interesting.

B
The guy is more or less my boss.

A
It was a moment. Forget it. Move on.

B
Yeah, well use your sense of humor on your own time.

A
It was a joke, an entertainment, don't get your underwear in a twist.

B
Do not play around with my life.

A
Humorless.

B
Thoughtless fool.

A
Get off it.

USAGE

You could request a version with one build or even a version with two. Give the actors ten minutes to learn the exercise and ten minutes to choose the build or builds and then present. After the exercise is complete, you could use the same text and ask for a single longer build, say six lines. Or you could ask for a second try choosing different sections.

COACHING
    Remind them that the build should coincide with what the actors feel is the crucial center of the scene. Remind them that if the build does not close the scene that it provides them with an earned pause after the build has been completed. As with all of these craft exercises, the actor must back them up with a psychology and belief or else they are of no use. A good comment is often, "You fulfilled the externals of the exercise, but I don't believe you." *Craft is the heart's handmaiden, no more.* In the above exercise, I would personally think that a build is useful from "at least it was funny" through "How about because it's a lie." The last four lines are another good choice. You will often have to mention that the build started too high and thus became extreme. Builds are best started in a normal tone and developed to a top well short of shouting.

Lay On, Lay Off

This is rather simple, really, but quite useful. It is a tool of rhythm and should probably be included in a section on those indispensable skills. To work with this craft tool, the student must first practice cuing tightly. Let's start there.

EXERCISE
    A
    Look, it's a family thing.

    B
    No more.

USAGE
    Yes, a two sentence exercise. Actor B literally cues off the sound of the "g" in actor A's closing word "thing." There is not a scintilla of space between the end of a line one and the beginning of line two. However, actor A's line is not cut off. We hear the "g."

COACHING
    Most people can do this immediately, but, as a veteran of thousands of classes, not everyone. Repetition solves all here. Before going onto the next exercise, make every class member do the two line exercise at least twice. The next exercise is more of the same in a four-line format. Both actors jump on the cues.

EXERCISE
    A
    Look, it's a family thing.

B
No more.

A
Granddad in World War II, Dad in Korea.

B
Stop.

COACHING

The obvious, right? Did they pick up the cues without cutting off any part of the other person's last word? This exercise is a good one to start off a class session with. Everyone enjoys it, everyone can do it, no one minds the repetition. Now, let's change the rules a little. Here's a six line exercise. Each actor jumps the first line they hear (tight cuing) and lays off the second, etc. To lay off, you take and fill a two beat pause (a thousand one, a thousand two). So...

A
Look, it's a family thing.

B
(Tight cue.)
No more.

A
(Tight cue.)
Granddad in World War II, Dad in Korea.

B
(Two beat pause.)
Stop.

A
(Two beat pause.)
I would appreciate you getting off my case.

B
(Tight cue.)
Leave the family out of it.

Usage

The point is to do the above exercise following the stage directions to the letter.

Coaching

Some actors have such a rapid metabolisms that they invariably make two beat pauses one beat long. Others make two beat pauses three beats long. Insist on the described at length of pause. Now let's vary the exercise.

Exercise

A
Look, it's a family thing.

B
(Two beat pause.)
No more.

A
(Two beat pause.)
Granddad in World War II, Dad in Korea.

B
(Tight cue.)
Stop.

A
(Tight cue.)
I would appreciate you getting off my case.

B
(Two beat pause.)
Leave the family out of it.

Usage

The cue pick-up, varied in this way, becomes a tool of interpretation and forces the actor to vary the thought process. Obviously, one doesn't do such a thing over the long haul. Someone who did it in a two character play for 90 minutes should be carted off to the madhouse, probably with an equally deranged audience. The tight cuing can always find use here and there and the "laying on, laying off" can enrich the psychology and rhythmic interest of a section here or there.

Coaching

The acting necessity is that pauses created by laying off must be psychologically filled. In the exercise, keep a close eye on the actors to make sure the pauses aren't empty. If they are, you can either suggest what the through process might be or, better still, make them do the exercise and say their thought process for the pause out loud (and then have them do it again in silence), or simply say, "The pause is empty, do it again." Oddly enough, the third method often works. Now, let's do one more exercise where the pair of actors use their own judgment as to where they lay on and where they lay off.

Exercise

A
Look, it's a family thing.

B
No more.

A
Granddad in World War II, Dad in Korea.

B
Stop.

A
I would appreciate you getting off my case.

B
Leave the family out of it, you're obsessed.

A
And you never talk about your family. Why is that?

B
Because they died in a head-on collision, does that explain it?

A
I'm really sorry. I didn't know.

B
Well, you do now.

A
Yes.

COACHING
As this is the fifth exercise, they've got it by now. You can say to a pair having just done the exercises, "Now spontaneously do it again ... differently." Usually they accomplish this without great difficulty, which allows you to make the point that all craft starts out mechanically but later becomes spontaneous. The actor will eventually be able to make use of all this work throughout the book without any pre-planning, i.e. it simply becomes acting.

Doing Things

Behavior

Many of our exercises have dealt with *doing*. Behavior is what the actor *does* while acting and how that assists the text and believability. It is, of course, theatrical to do nothing, to simply stand, to use stillness to express any number of states, but, were we to study the plays we see and convert that to statistics, I think we would find that over 80% of the time the actor is *doing* something. What the actor does is behavior. A great problem in acting training is that very often there is nothing to *do* in the classroom. There are no staircases, no formal gardens, no dining room tables, no costumes, no (or few) props, and thus, very little to *do*. The actor who works in a classroom with no doors open, no tea to serve, no smooth rocks to pick up, no champagne glasses or coffee tables, learns to think of acting as *not* doing and often the acting seems somehow without detail, and detail is acting's richest vein. A good acting book could be written on the actor's behavior alone, and a damn thick one at that. Here it can be only one of our concerns, a starved version so to speak, but we can introduce (or remind) the actor of this fascinating and necessary part of their work. Let's try couple of categories:

1. Behavior that completes. Making, pouring, and drinking coffee. Tying a shoe. Typing and sending an e-mail. The actor moves towards completion whether he/she completes or not.
2. Emotion driven behavior. Throwing down a vase and shattering it. Punching the air. Flinging yourself on a sofa. Smashing your fist against your forehead.
3. Nervous behavior. Compulsively smoothing your dress. Idly cleaning cat hair from your suit.

Playing with your hair.
4. All of the above. The three categories above are often part of the behavioral mix, as in: A man is tying his shoe while he speaks (completed behavior). He stops momentarily, brushes his hair back and drums his fingers on his knee (nervous behavior). He starts on the shoe again, but suddenly, in a rage, throws the shoe against the wall (emotional behavior).

Try it!

Usage

There are other categories, but working with these three will remind the actor that acting is *doing* and that doing creates believability and often informs character and text. Because of the hundreds of thousands of behaviors available, we cannot train the actor as we can in mastering the double take. We can only make the actor more aware of the possibilities. Behavior is something more than a technique, and yet it can be practiced.

Let's do an exercise for each of the categories. First, completed behavior. The actor sits at a table and writes the letter, puts it in an envelope, licks and closes the envelope. Writes an address, puts a stamp on.

A
(Talks as he writes. B listens.)
So this guy keys my car. I happened to turn back, I see him. I yell suitable obscenities. He says in somewhat more colorful language, "You parked with three inches clearance on the driver's side, Jerk off!" Then he picks up a rock and turns my front window into a spider web and walks off. Clever coward that I am, I follow, I get his license number. I have now written the police asking that he be put into a cell with the vipers, spiders, and bears. This is called polite and appropriate revenge. I could've told my mother who

would have found his house and stabbed him to death with her onyx letter opener.

(He tosses the letter on the table, stands up, pushes chair in, and leaves.)

USAGE

A long enough exercise to be given to be learned outside of class. We will use it for all four categories. This week demands the actual props. The actor will probably find that some of the behavior must be done in pauses so as to time the whole so he/she has finished stamping the letter just as the speech finishes, which is the goal.

COACHING

Remind the actors that the business *(writing the letter, etc)* also parses the text as in: "I yell suitable obscenities *(finishes writing.)* He says, in somewhat more colorful language... *(puts cap on pen.)* You parked with three inches clearance on the driver's side, Jerk off! *(Tosses pen on table)*, etc. Also, be prepared for some students needing to repeat the exercises two or three times to finish the business at the right time in the dialogue. If someone simply cannot do so, rather than feeling the failure, tell them to practice at home and "Do it tomorrow." The actors will see how this directed behavior enhances their concentration and, when they've got it down, their confidence. They may be making strategic mistakes you can help them with, such as spending too long writing and then having to fold, insert, lick, and stamp in a frantic panic. There is also the key matter of the character's attitude toward the business. Done angrily, it's one thing; done ceremoniously, it's another. It's a good time to discuss how crucial the character's attitude always is toward the line in the activity. I often say, "I hear the line, what's the attitude?" Now let's use the same text again, keeping the same business that needs to be completed, but add a couple pieces of "emotional" behavior.

Usage

This time the actor needs to add an interior life wrestling with anger toward the person who shattered the window during the speech. This could result in a number of behaviors being added to the details of getting the letter ready, such as…
1. Being clumsy with the props because you are so angry.
2. Taking anger out on the props. Smacking the letter with your fist. Picking up and shaking the devil out of the letter itself.
3. Throwing the pen when finished.
4. Getting up and sitting down again in an agitated manner.

Etc, etc, etc. For the sake of the exercise, each actor should add three (no more) details that exemplify some emotional state suitable to the material.

Usage

So, the actor is to handle the letter business plus add behavior proceeding from the emotional state.

Coaching

Before repeating the exercise, it might help to provide a bit of back-story. A and B are siblings and know each other's foibles well. B does not interfere with A's rant but is sympathetic, feeling A's need to vent but will eventually calm down. A is particularly upset because he had saved for some time to buy the car, making many economies. He was planning to drive down to his parents' on the coming weekend to show them his purchase. As his father considers him careless, it will now be an embarrassing trip. A has also been trying to rid himself of a nasty temper, so getting upset further upsets him still. In this second take on performing the piece, the coach must note if it is emotionally believable. For the sake of this exercise, the emotional state must result in visible behavior. Has the actor successfully blended the two behaviors?

Now, on to the third version of behavior to blend with the other two. This is nervous and or unconscious behavior. Let's break that down a little:
1. Behavior that deals with actor's own body or clothes such as buttoning or unbuttoning the top button of a shirt or blouse. Adjusting clothing for comfort. Playing with a ring. Setting one's watch. Kicking off one's shoes, playing with your hair.
2. Almost unconscious behavior that seems without a logic connected to the situation. Feeling the texture of a table, snapping your fingers, chewing your lip, tapping your foot, rubbing your wrists together, and on, and on.

All right, let's add this third and more abstract behavior score to the original monologue. To recap, we now have the following categories present:
1. Completed behavior (making, pouring, and drinking coffee).
2. Emotional behavior (physical venting).
3. The physical minutia of life.

Let's do this thing.

USAGE

I would give the class the first half hour to go off in various corners of the room to rehearse this fairly complicated combination of elements.

COACHING

Because the entire enterprise of examining behavior is less a process of learning a technique and more one of an introduction to a lifetime of practice, I would suggest to the instructor that this final take on the exercise should be more a matter of praise than censure and used as a mere example of what behavior is rather than a how-to lesson. You might remind him also that if this were simply a class on "behavior," we would now add stillness and austerity to the mix. We are trying to lodge a splinter in their head ("Oh! So I don't just stand there!") and hope it endures in their work.

Clean and Dirty

These, in my view, are crucial skills for the young actor. *When we talk about clean, we mean a physical precision that makes the text paramount while still providing a believable physical score.* The more complex the language, as in Stoppard, Wilde, Shaw, and Shakespeare, the "cleaner" the work should be to protect and parse the script. Let me suggest a very short exercise to make clear what is meant by clean.

EXERCISE
(Onstage a single chair. The actor stands beside it.)

A
So, I guess I came to tell you this.

(The actor sits immediately after the line.)

You know what I'm going to say but I need to say it.

(Crosses legs.)

I loved you, you know that, but that's done now.

(Uncrosses legs.)

There's no more to it than that.

(Rises but does nothing beyond that.)

I'll get my stuff out of here tomorrow.

(Moves behind chair.)

I think you need to say something now.

(Places both hands on chair back and leans forward.)

Usage

The point here is that the physicality takes place in the moments when the actor isn't speaking so the text is still in the clear.

Coaching

For the sake of the exercise, the teacher must insist on each of the physical moments above being done precisely. There is to be no talking when moving but as soon as the move is complete, the speech resumes. I often say, "The move behind the chair starts immediately after the word 'tomorrow.'" You should also discourage any physicality not stated in the exercise. No gesturing. No scratching. No taking off coats, etc. You should also mention that we are doing an exaggerated version of "clean" so that the concept is understood. When the above exercise has been done to the teacher's satisfaction, let's try another.

Usage

This next exercise uses the physical elements of the first, all of which must be completed during the new exercise, in order, but the student choose where to place them. The physical elements chronologically are:
1. The actor stands beside a chair.
2. The actor sits in the chair.
3. The actor crosses his/her legs.
4. The actor rises from the chair.
5. The actor moves behind the chair.
6. The actor puts both hands on the chair back and leans forward.

Now, the actor does the following monologue using the movements to parse the speech clearly.

EXERCISE
A
It is murderously hot out there. Could I have a drink of water? There's a cat out there keeled over, a cat with sunstroke. Ok, I don't, can't, understand why we have to stay here? We've still got the four thousand dollars and the car. The cops have no idea what state we're in, and they can't even prove there has been a crime. Please, let's pack up; let's roll.

COACHING
Tell the actors this speech has the same number of sentences as the first exercise so they can solve the problem by only moving in the space between sentences. On the other hand, they could skip a sentence and make two moves (in order) the next time they encounter a period. So it might go:

"There's a cat out there keeled over with sunstroke. Look, I don't, can't, understand why we have to stay here?"

(The actor crosses his legs and then uncrosses them.)

The obvious point is that we don't have to devise a movement to be done every time there's a period. That would, frankly, begin to look robotic. Now keeping the same physical score, have the actors repeat the second exercise putting two physical actions together at points of their own choosing until they run out. They then hold the final position until the speech ends. Is the speech still clean? Yes it is. The point here is that at a natural stopping point in the text there could be a series of activities. As in:

A
You're going to tell me you don't have it, right?

(Opens drawer, rummages throughout. Dumps it out on floor. Replaces and closes drawer.)

You have one minute to tell me where it is.

To let the actors feel what this is like, do the following short exercise.

A
It is murderously hot out there. Could I have a drink of water? There's a cat out there keeled over, a cat with sunstroke.

(Sits in chair. Crosses and uncrosses his legs. Rises and moves behind the char. Puts both hands on chair back and leans forward.)

Look, I don't understand why we have to stay here.

USAGE
This hopefully makes clear to the actors that I am not suggesting a physical action after every sentence.

EXERCISE
A
Look,

(The actor sits in the chair.)

I don't,

(Crosses legs.)

can't,

(Uncrosses legs.)

understand why we have to stay here.

(Stands up.)

Usage
This clarifies the idea that you can break up the text at logical places other than the period and still work clearly.

Coaching
You might mention to the actors that physical moves that cleanly parse the text can be very small. To demonstrate this, you might use the following short exercise:

Exercise
You are…

(Glances up at the sky.)

clumsier than a hog on ice.

(Glances left.)

That vase belonged to my Great Grandmother.

(Looks directly at the offender.)

It's the only thing I had of hers.

(Clenches a fist.)

Coaching
Here the physicality is small. Make sure the actor keeps it that way. The same end of protecting the text while maintaining a physical life is achieved. Have them parse the following short piece with very small movements while sitting in a chair.

EXERCISE

> A
>
> I don't know how the dog got out. I'm pretty sure I never opened a door. I watched T.V. that's all. The dog was on the sofa. He jumped down and headed for the back door. Maybe a half hour later I went to check on him. All the doors were closed, he was gone.

COACHING

Insist on the movements being small and not wildly dramatic. Say "smaller" and ask to see the exercise again. Continue to ask for smaller until you like the level.

USAGE

By now the idea of "clean" should have penetrated the class. Remind them that they have been working on clarifying and protecting the text while acting. Now tell them that dirty is the opposite of what they have been doing.

Go back to the first exercise in the section. The one that starts, "So I guess I came to tell you this." This exercise should now be repeated. In the first go-round, there was a physical action played at the end of each sentence and no physicality elsewhere. The result? Clean. Clean to the point of obsessive. Let's now handle that exercise very differently. There are six sentences. Let's break those up into two units.

EXERCISE

> *(Onstage a single chair. The actor stands beside it. He/she fans themselves.)*
>
> A
>
> So, I guess I came to tell you this. You know what I'm going to say but I need to say it. I loved you, you know that, but that's done now.
>
> *(The actor sits in the middle of the last sentence, not at the end)*

There's no more to it than that. I'll get my stuff out of here tomorrow. I think you need to say something now.

USAGE

We are using this second go at the same exercise to do something dramatically opposed. *We are not protecting the text with our physicality. We are invading it... even distracting from it.* Before, the only physicality fell at the punctuation, perhaps at the period. Now, whatever physicality the actor uses should fall in the middle of the line. Better still, other behavior should be added. Perhaps the actor twirls a keychain during the lines or brushes her hair. While the text becomes less important, the sense of reality the actor brings is enhanced.

COACHING

Steer the actor clear of what we are calling "clean." *Keep his physicality away from the start or end of the line.* Add behavior that has a continuous nature while it is being completed such as carefully folding a piece of paper into eighths, eating a banana, getting a sliver out of an index finger, etc. When each class member has completed the "dirty" exercise, initiate a class conversation about the difference between "clean" and "dirty." Stay away from value judgments, but encourage feelings about the impact of both. A reminder that any technique exercise is likely to have a slightly mechanical tinge when first undertaken and before it is absorbed by the actor and backed up with a belief in the situation. Let's try another dirty exercise with two actors.

EXERCISE

A
You invited who? I've got like fifteen things I have to get... They never go home, do you realize that. They're like statues. I have got to get some sleep tonight.

B
You've heard of networking, this is networking. They know Ray Fisher and Fisher knows what's-his-name Morgan and Morgan can get you an interview with André Zvonereva.

A
Man, you are a careerist machine! Worse, it's all a fantasy. Zvonereva is not giving some just graduated person the time of day. Jeeze!

B
You prefer to be hopeless? Fine. I however am having them over. I am going to smile and have a career. You can sit around and stew in idealism.

COACHING
Remember, this is "dirty" work. Suggest they use run-on sentences or even do a whole speech in a gulp. They should walk, tie their shoes, scribble on a notepad during the speeches. They should not worry about distracting from the text. In fact, such distraction is a point of the exercise. *Disregarding punctuation, pursuing stage business during the lines, sitting, getting up, and walking while speaking are the very nature of "dirty."*

USAGE
Now have them re-do the same four line sequence as "clean." We know from past experience this means saving important pieces of physicality for moments of punctuation or places where you want to give particular emphasis. For instance, in B's first line, B might start sitting. At the end of "You've heard of networking, this is networking," he might rise and go behind the chair before speaking. When he is still (as in motionless), he would say the next line. If B wishes to break up a line, putting focus on a moment within it, he could do the following:

B
...and Morgan can get you an interview with

(He pauses, folding his arms and then says:)

André Zvonereva.

In "clean," physicality is the handmaiden of text, not it's equal.

COACHING
When they attempt to clean up their dirty work in this exercise, insist they limit any physicality to moments when they aren't speaking. Be rigorous.

USAGE
Now we get to the real point of "clean" and "dirty:" in practically all cases, we use a mix.

EXERCISE EXAMPLE
(Monologue. But it should be said to another student sitting with his or her back to us, the audience, but facing the speaker.)

(A stands with hands clasped behind his back.)

A
Yeah, what else is new?

(Puts hands on top of his head.)

Since I was born we've been in and out of recessions, and in-between, hey, we've had unsustainable growth.

(Takes hands down, sits in chair. Once in the chair, he conducts his own speech with his hands as if the speech was a musical score.)

Personally, I'm a big fan of unsustainable growth, it gives me caviar, extremely luxurious cars and lovers lined up around the block begging for my body.

(He becomes completely still.)

Unsustainable growth is the way to go.

(He crosses his legs.)

You strike me as more of a recession personality.

(He snaps his fingers.)

USAGE

Have the students do this exercise with the exact blocking and business mentioned and *nothing else*. You can see from the work, they are mixing "clean" and "dirty."

COACHING

Remind the actor that "clean" moves physicality away from the text. In a certain sense, we have text *then* we have physicality. Let me again illustrate this with a single sentence. "I don't care, really, no kidding, just tell me what you did?" In working clean, we have activity and behavior, but it is all between pieces of text. As in: I don't care *(actor sits)* really, *(runs hands through hair)* no kidding *(crosses legs)*, just tell me what you did? *(actor sucks on thumb.)* In dirty, text and physicality are concurrent. As in: during whole sentence, the actor unwraps a candy bar and eats it. Make sure the actor fully understands the difference. Now, a final exercise for two actors to mix dirty and clean.

EXERCISE

A

So I come home and she's on the couch in one of my old shirts, weeping. Apparently, much to my surprise, ballet companies fire for gaining weight.

B
You are kidding me, she is like a pencil lead. She eats parsley as an entrée. She gained how much weight?

A
Three pounds. Can you believe that? The ballet warden, or whatever you call her, keeps a scale in her shoulder bag astoundingly enough. So this Captain Bly of the ballet marches into the middles of a dress rehearsal, slaps down the scale, grabs Sal by the ear and discovers the dastardly poundage. Then she is marched out of the theatre still in her swan tutu and deposited in the street.

B
My God, that is, I don't know what that is, that is ghastly. Poor Sal, she only danced, we both know she has no life. She doesn't even want a life. She could... there's no telling... this is like suicide watch time. She's at your place? What are those people she works for, master of the dark arts? Okay. I'll go over there. Call Gretchen. Sal loves Gretchen. Tell her to meet me. Are you out of your mind to leave her alone?

USAGE
Set this final exercise in a place where there is plenty of behavior available. A kitchen would be good. Make props part of the exercise. If not in a kitchen, maybe at lunch in a restaurant or getting ready to play tennis. The props will assist with both dirty and clean. This exercise is long enough that you may want to hand it out the day before for memorization.

COACHING
Suggest that the piece be preponderantly "dirty," with key moments or sections of "clean." As this is in a sense a

quiz or exam on "clean and dirty," give them a longer rehearsal period. Perhaps a whole class is devoted to rehearsal with the performance given the day after. To ensure group learning, suggest the watchers clench their right hand into a fist during "clean" and raise that same hand during "dirty." *You might emphasize that eventually the actor doesn't "plan" clean or dirty, but being familiar with these possibilities can use them spontaneously to enhance their work.* Remind them one more time that this concept is simply a tool and is best used sparingly to solve acting problems as they arise.

SMALL, MEDIUM, BIG

In my years of teaching, I've noticed that the actors (quite sensibly) size their performances to the room. The problem lies in the fact that they spend years in that room and thus, habitually, work in the same size. Part of the sizing depends, of course, on the auditorium and the number of seats. A larger problem has to do with the fact that each actor tends to feel comfortable at a certain size and spends far too much time there, sacrificing the vocal variety that could greatly enhance their work. *Young actors working to be both honest and believable find early on that it's easier to be truthful if you play small.* The following exercises make clear for the actor the different impact and sense each size provides a given piece of material and the value of mixing sizes regardless of the number of seats. The words small, medium, and big are relative. Let's just say that "small" is a natural, un-pushed tone without a lot of support. "Medium" has a sense of being "pushed out" a little, of speaking to someone several feet away, and "large" is... well, large. A strongly supported tone with significant vocal energy. It isn't shouting, but it is the next step down. In the first exercise, the actor should do it three times: small, medium, and large.

A

I just want to get out of here, the whole state is claustrophobic. Too many trees, too many egos, way too much self-satisfaction, way too much Nordic restraint. I want open, I want to see fifteen miles, I want larger emotions, I want out-of-control. I want love, hate, jealousy, warmth, anything but this damn logic and common sense. Let me out of here.

Coaching

A lot will depend on where the actor starts with "small." If "small" is actually "medium," then large will be yelling and that's not what we are looking for. You will doubtless have to stop certain actors and get them to start over. Medium can only be described in relationship to the other two. If we were using seats as a measure, then small would be heard throughout a hundred and fifty seat house, medium would serve a five hundred seater, and big would play for a thousand. You will need to insist that the actor play a strong action or objective and then hold that action steady through the three exercises. *You will also need to contain the actor when playing large because it isn't shouting. "Large" still keeps something in reserve.* A good way to respond is to tell the actor what you are receiving in each case as in: "Your small seems intimate and searching and very believable. In the medium, it seems more intellectual, more objective. Almost a sense of lecturing. Perhaps a business relationship safer than a marriage. The large seems more like a barely contained anger..." etc. Then ask the actor what they felt doing the exercise. Did size affect their interior life? Did it change the action? Is large sustainable for a whole scene? What did size make them feel about their relationship to the other person? Remind them that the point of this particular exercise is to stay locked in to a single size and not to vary it. This leads directly into the next exercise where variation of size is the whole point.

Exercise

A

Upset? Yes, I'm upset, and no it's not just a simple jealousy. It's the lying and the subterfuge over how long, six months, eight? A day I could put up with, maybe a week, that could still be an impulse playing itself out, but not this. Did you think of me? Did I cross your mind and then you decided, "Hey, this feels good, I'll just go with it and let the chips fall where they will?" Well they did, the chips fell and

I'm out of here. Don't even bother to say anything. It's over.

Usage

You will find that some actors have almost no sense of size, and in this exercise you will not be able to tell the difference between small and large. If this is true, have them repeat the exercise until you can clearly tell the difference. Then go back to the exercise and request that the actor now add "medium" so all three sizes are represented in the monologue. You may want to give the class five minutes to rehearse. Now when you watch the exercise again, insist on all three sizes being present and do not let them sit down until they are. They will now begin to see that the variety in size shapes the speech and even forces the actor to provide a real thought process. Because the exercise is difficult for some, you should do another exercise in the same way.

Exercise

A

Look, I don't know where we are. How would I know that? We're visiting your American Gothic parents in Corn Row, Kansas or whatever and if we missed some turnoff past grain silo number two thousand and seven, I can't help you out. Why you dragged me down here I have no idea. Why? Why? I don't find it charming, I don't find it exotic, and it doesn't remind me of *To Kill a Mockingbird* or *The Last Picture Show*. Actually, it bores me to the point of being suicidal. So, you figure out where we are. Leave me out of it… permanently.

Coaching

You want to see (or rather, hear) all three sizes. You might want to tell the actor to start with small or big because the middle range is best handled comparatively. It's also helpful to the understanding if you have them return at the end of the category they began with. You will doubtless need to point out that we have to believe how they got from small to big or the reverse. When a moment, or speech, or scene moves from small to big, there is usually a conscious restraint inside the small; he or she is restraining the big as long as possible, until the feelings that drive the big can no longer be constrained. Sometimes small to medium to big is very much like the builds we have already worked on; I have found that after doing the two exercises provided here, I ask them to use the concept in an audition piece they have been performing for some time, which they invariably find interesting and helpful. The idea of these three categories needs repetition and should probably cover several days in class.

Props in Eight

I have thought for years that one of the great failures in most actor training is the simple unavailability of props. *In a lot of the acting classes I have visited, there is very little for the actor to do and very little to do it with.* Young actors who don't have cups and saucers and beer bottles and baseball bats and mirrors and lipsticks available during their scene work get used to acting without behavior, and it is behavior that gives performance its crucial detail. Now the exercise I'm about to describe devolves from that. Don't waste the props you have. If you are seated at a table and there are teacups, saucers, and a teapot available, you don't want to be done delivering the tea after the first two lines. Break down your use of the prop into several beats as in:

Lydia
I know you don't have long.

(Touches the teapot and finds it hot.)

It's very kind of you to take this time with me.

(Places the tea cup and saucer in front of him.)

You knew Jack well, I think.

(Places her own cup. Finds a speck on her saucer which she removes with a careful finger.)

You were both in Georgia last December, were you not?

(Picks up the teapot.)

No, I'm wrong, it was in Rhode Island…

(Lost in though, puts the pot back down.)

Or was it the job in Oregon? You travel so much for the company.

(Notices the pot has left a damp spot. Wipes it with her napkin.)
I am right am I not…

(Puts napkin back on her lap.)

You do know Jack?

(Feels the pot again. Finds the temperature adequate.)

Of course you do.

(Pours his tea.)

He sends me postcards, I have a drawer-full.

(Pours her own tea.)

I often wish I had traveled more than I do.

(Puts pot down.)

I should get to the point, shouldn't I?

(Sips her tea.)

I'm just enjoying having a visitor.

(Wipes lips with napkin.)

Tell me about Jack.

(Puts napkin back on lap.)

   Some of this business will be done on the line and some off. Putting down the teapot might make a sound that punctuates the end of the line, etc. *The obvious point is that there is more behavior available than simply grabbing a pot and pouring the tea.* Let me give you another example

   A
Sorry to bother you. You know what I mean?

(Reaches back to take out wallet. Realizes his hand may be dirty.)

You're a busy person, I'm a busy person.

(Rubs hands together.)

The deal here is…

(Examines hands.)

That you may have some knowledge…

(Takes wallet out.)

Of what went down Thursday. You know, last Thursday.

(Takes several cards out of the wallet. Retains cards, puts down wallet.)

And I'd have to say…

(Begins to go through cards as he speaks.)
We are at, what you might call, an impasse. No suspects, short on evidence, not I might say on top of the situation.

(Finds card. Puts it down.)

So we're kind of flailing around here.

(Puts other cards back I wallet.)

Which brings me to my point. Such as it is.

(Puts wallet back in pocket.)

I was wondering…

(Pushes card over to Jane.)

Well, hoping as much as wondering;

(Reverses card so it's facing her.)

If you knew this guy…

(Pushes card even closer to her.)

Take a good look.

    Which gets more mileage out of the prop then simply taking out the wallet and handing over the card.
    The actor needs to think creatively as to how much or how little behavior a prop will bear inside the given circumstances of the scene. Additionally, I am suggesting that the actor break down the props usage into counts much in the same way that stage combat is choreographed. The lesson to be learned is that almost every piece of prop-driven behavior has several parts and the business can be expanded to assist the actor over a longer period of time.

Exercise

Here are two pieces of text. I leave the nature of the props and the activity to those in the class. The goal is to break the completion of the action implied by the props into either four, six, or eight counts.

A

I don't know what his phone number is and, hey, frankly I could care less. You're the one who got me into this and as far as I'm concerned you're the one who's going to get me out. So what I'm saying here is, you're the one who's going to make the call, not me. I'm not making the call, so get off your butt and get this over with. Do it now.

Usage

Each class member could try using the prop decided on and its behavior broken down first into four counts and then into eight counts. Sometimes, the actor will need the repetition of doing it more than once. An advanced version of the exercise is to then put the beats back into continuous action so the business is not simply doled out of the moments of punctuation. You can come up with dozens of prop activities. Here are five:
1. Tennis shoes are put on, laced and tied during the speech.
2. Street makeup is applied.
3. A glass of milk or juice is poured and consumed.
4. A newspaper is searched for a given article and then given to the other actor to read.
5. Silverware is examined to make sure it is clean before eating with it.

Exercise Two

A

I cannot believe this! You are telling me the guy busted me with my own brother, while he's the one who suggested it? What gives him the right, huh? He knows… you know he knows… what will happen now. My brother will go absolutely crazy, and that's for starters. He is not a rational person, my brother, okay? I cannot believe I have to deal with this now. I don't have time for this. Look, I want to talk to this guy, you understand me? This was going to be a terrific day. How does this happen to me?

USAGE
Same intent in terms of the prop. *The ideal is a prop that has a functional use.* Keys that open a door. A can of Coke you drink. A tie you tie. The exercise can also be done with an actor simply playing with a parcel, but the actor benefits if the prop can be used and the use completed. It is possible that the instructor might start with the actors using one of the illustrated speeches (done as written) and then move onto the exercises where the actor creates the business. I would assume that this problem work would fill at least two classes of an hour or more and easily three. In all cases, it is good if the speaker has a listener. An advanced usage might be the listener being the one who handles the prop.

Coaching
When breaking the use of the prop into counts, we must always remember that then thought behind the speech is more important than pouring the tea. Keep reminding the actor that the thought is primary and pouring the tea is secondary. Can the actor do the speech so that that physical business is background rather than foreground? Cant he physical action be responsible to the actor's thought process and, in fact, make that thought process clearer? Ask the actor to repeat the exercise until the thought process dominates.

CHOREOGRAPHING BEHAVIOR

Young actors often freeze onstage. Their circumstance of being watched sends their self consciousness into orbit. In the most extreme cases, all behavior stops and, except for breathing, nothing moves. If a fly landed on their noses, they wouldn't brush it off. If ice cream had dripped on the chair they're about to sit in, they wouldn't wipe it off. As I was writing the above, I paused to think. I sat back in my chair and looked at the ceiling. I adjusted the watch on my arm, scratched my itchy moustache, put down my pen, flexed my slightly arthritic right hand, picked up the pen, and continued writing (yes, I don't use a computer). These are the very behaviors that give acting its compelling detail and they are the very behavior that the actors self consciousness erodes.

Sometimes it's useful, even necessary, to choreograph behavior. I will venture that every professional actor sometimes resorts to it. I provide this apology for the exercise because it will be thought to be at cross purposes with the actors' spontaneity and even their "honesty." Pay no attention to it; it's a time honored process. It won't hurt to play with the idea.

As in: A man or woman sits waiting to be called into the boss's office. Will it be praise or blame? Is their job on the line here? From inside the office, we hear the boss finishing up an extremely unpleasant phone call. You are the only person on stage. You've got about fifteen seconds to fill before the boss calls you in. What to do? ("Do," by the way, is the perfect question.) Now, in such an exercise, the given circumstances obviously give us our playing field. If you're on crutches, it's one thing; if you've spilled soup on your shirt, it's another. If you're having an affair with the

boss (perhaps recently consummated in that very office), it will impact the choreography. But let's keep this simple. You need to choreograph fifteen seconds of acting. Let's posit, for the sake of argument, six activities:
1. You look to your left at an imaginary clock.
2. You look back, noticing there are some crumbs on your clothes from a muffin you ate for lunch. You brush them off.
3. You catch the receptionist looking at you.
4. You smile at her.
5. You adjust your sitting position to look more relaxed.
6. You inhale and exhale three times slowly to calm yourself down.

At this point, the boss calls you in. You now have a physical (and hopefully psychological) structure to fill the time. Now try it. Try it again. Try it a third time. Make sure you get and give the necessary physical information. Really see the time on the clock before you look away. Get all those crumbs off. Smile at the receptionist. Hold the smile. Now move on to the next thing. You have more than fifteen seconds of material? Take a unit out. You still have time to fill? Add a unit. Remember, you could do six entirely different things, all this is a work in progress. You're just giving yourself the security of a structure.

USAGE
In this case, it was to fill a given period of stage time. There could also be a physical score that accompanies a speech (we'll try that in a minute), or a physical score for an important transition, or a physical score while you listen to someone else (we'll try that in a moment). *Am I suggesting that every moment of the play should be so scored? Good God, no! A* thousand times, no. I'm talking about situations where you feel uncomfortable without behavior. You also may start with a score for a moment or section and then simply handle the moment spontaneously when you feel more com-

fortable and "inside" the role. Too much of this work would feel mechanical and seem mechanical. Used judiciously and well, however, no one will ever know.

EXERCISE

We're going to score an important transition. In this case, a silent moment when the character prepares internally for something crucial they need to say.

> A
> Listen, thanks, I really appreciate the coffee. I kind of gave up caffeine but guess what? I'm back. I'm glad you agreed to see me. I didn't know if you would.
>
> *(Now you're internally preparing a difficult moment.*
> *Let's try a structure of three:*
> *Runs hand through hair.*
> *Taps table twice with forefinger.*
> *Crosses arms over chest.)*
>
> I'd like to try again. Us. I'd like to give it another try. I know you think I'm crazy.

First do the exercise using the written structure. Then do it again with your own structure of three. Then do it again trying a two and a four.

EXERCISE

Now we're going to try scoring a whole speech physically. This exercise blurs the line between scoring and blocking.

A: So, I finally said, "What the hell, I'll just take it over to him." I told myself I'd do it Tuesday and I did. He's got a big place, maybe an acre of ground. Intimidating. I almost left, but finally I rang the bell. He answered... he's a big guy, maybe 6'3", at least 250. I said, "I think maybe you dropped this." Then I handed him the bills in an envelope. Went completely pale. The guy almost fainted. Asked me where I got it? "Wouldn't you like to know?" I said. Then I kind of sauntered off.

Score: Stands behind chair leaning on it. Takes off jacket, hangs it on back of chair. Moves around to front of chair and sits. Leans back, puts hands behind head. Rubs hands together. Takes off glasses. Puts glasses in pocket.

Do the exercise a second time, making the physical work more organic. Now write out your own physical score (careful you don't do too much or make it too eccentric). Show this new work to the class.

EXERCISE

This time, we're going to structure a physical score for use while listening. Actors should pair up. Each learns the speech. One does the speech while the other performs the score. The two actors then reverse roles.

("A" sits in a chair. The listening actor stands.)

A	Listener
I don't think you're going to like this but, frankly, that's no longer my priority. I think you have to give Henry back the dog, man. He loves that dog... more than me he loves that dog. Listen up, man, he asked you to watch the dog while he was on vacation, not take the dog out to your father's farm. Give him back the dog.	*(Tries to remove a small splinter at the knuckle joint of the index finger.)* *(Stretches, eyes on the speaker.)* *(Eyes on his shoes. Moves one foot experimentally.)* *(Puts hands on top of head.)* *(Relaxed, hands at his side.)*

USAGE

The physical score given is intentionally random. The point is that behavior doesn't completely stop while we listen. Our listening score shouldn't be intrusive. On the other hand, you don't have to turn into a pillar of salt to avoid taking focus. Sometimes, you have to score a set of behavior if you are feeling stymied or self-conscious. You can lose them when you find you don't need them anymore. Each actor should do the above exercise twice with the written score. Then, each pair can be given ten minutes to provide their own listening score that they feel is psychologically apt in the given circumstances.

EXERCISE

(This is another piece of dialogue for the listener to score.)

A
Look, I'm sorry if I woke you up. It's what, two, three in the morning? But you said if I decided I should tell you. I decided. I want to get re-married. I'm ready. I really am. So, sorry to wake you but you said. What do you think? What's your reaction? Want me to make you a cup of coffee?

Coaching
Does the score seem natural as behavior? Do you take it to be in the character's emotional ballpark? Is it too busy? Does one piece of physicality transition naturally into the next? If it is a transitional score, is it too long or too short? Does the actor fully commit to the behavior? Does the exercise need another repetition? Would it be valuable to switch partners and do the exercise again? Remember that learning needs sufficient repetition. Maybe the spoken speech is done too slowly and the behavior seems overextended. Don't jump past the actor trying to fulfill the written exercise score before simply doing their own. It should also be emphasized that behavior most certainly need not be choreographed. In most cases, we wish it to occur spontaneously. But sometimes…

The Illusion of the First Time

The land of spontaneity (or seeming spontaneity). Not only does the actor actually know what's next, she has practiced the "next" over and over again. How then to fool both yourself and the audience? As this is a book on craft, we will examine some craft solutions. Here's a speech.

A

I sat in the chair by the bed watching him sleep until I ached from sitting and then went out to the tool shed where I had hidden the suitcase and put it by the door of the car and stood without knowing what to do next in the yard, listening to the trucks go by on the freeway down below. I owed him a good solid ending, something clear, something logical, or emotional, but there wasn't a thing in my head. Nothing. No exit line. I walked the three miles to the bus station. Over it over. Sometimes there aren't words for it.

Usage

This is a long enough speech that it should be assigned overnight. Here are several ways to go about creating the illusion we seek.

1) Lost in the experience.

To do this you take a pause where you let your mind leave the present (and the speech) and go back to the past being described, so: take a pause after "put it by the door of the care and stood (without knowing what to do next")". In this pause, see, hear, and feel things you saw, heard, and felt then. Give yourself four or five seconds, then shake yourself awake and continue the speech. Everybody do it.

COACHING

Make sure there is some small physicality in the pause, perhaps a change of focus. If the pause extends more than five seconds, stop and start over. If the pause seems empty, ask what they are seeing and hearing. If they still have trouble, give them three concrete things to do in the pause. 1) Glance up at the moon. 2) Kick away a small rock. 3) Look at their hand. As soon as the three things are done, they must continue speaking. All in five seconds.

All right, now add number two. This is to pick the perfect phrase. The actor stops for a moment (a thousand one) and then very clearly articulates the next few words. As in: "I owned him a good solid ending…(now stop, briefly consider, and then present your perfect words) something clear, something logical or emotional…" (you need to pick these words as you say them). Add this to your previous work on the speech and do the work again.

COACHING

Insist on the small pause to pick the words and insist the words be presented decisively. Now let's add a third illusion. This is the doubling of a pronoun, as in "I…I walked the three miles to the bus station." Any pronoun will do, you are making a value judgment of what was done or said. Pick a pronoun, double it, and add it to your work on the speech. You are now including three techniques, 1) Lost in the experience, 2) Picking a perfect phrase, 3) Doubling a pronoun. Use them all.

Add number four. 4) Make a sentence completely rushed and unimportant, barely heard and very quick (see "Throwing Away the Line"). This should be a sentence the actor deems less important. One might be "…then went out to the tool shed where I had hidden the suitcase…" (only part of the sentence, I know). Another would be "I walked the three miles to the bus station." Add this on.

Coaching

Make sure the sentence is rushed and understated, maybe only half heard. Also make sure they have used the other three techniques.

Now one more: The Uh, Um, and Er. These are placeholder words we use while we think (not in Shakespeare or outside the mid-twentieth century). Add two (not more) placeholder words to the speech as in: "I sat in the chair by the bed, ummm, watching him sleep." Or, "No, uhhh, exit line." Pick your own. Now there are five techniques in play:

1) Lost in the experience.
2) The perfect phrase.
3) Doubling the pronoun or the connective.
4) Rushed and unimportant.
5) The un, um, er.

Now one more: The false finish. This is when you seem to finish the speech. Think you're done, and then one more thing comes to you. As in: "I walked the tree miles to the bus station." After the line, go on with life. Pick up your jacket or start for the door or go back to drinking your coffee. Then, suddenly, more words occur to you. In this case: "Over is over. Sometimes there aren't words for it."

When the actor adds this sixth flourish, make sure the speech seems OVER! Then make sure you see the next words occur. They are an addition. A new thought. When all six techniques have been practiced, give them a night or two to prepare the speech and present it. Because this whole exercise has only been an attempt to get the actors to think about the illusion of the first time, don't be too critical of the result. You might give them another go on a different speech in two week's time.

Taking the Arrow

The actor in training often reacts in the small to invisible range. They could be told the building was collapsing, a lion was in the closet, or their scene partner was a zombie, and they barely blink an eye. A little practice in opening up the reaction, going a touch further, while maintaining believability might be in order. The phrase "taking the arrow" is hopefully evocative. *There's the moment of impact, the pain, and the reaction to both the pain and the event.* Additionally, in terms of craft, there are times when it drives the play and reveals character to see response.

Usage

In the first exercise, the moment to take the arrow is starred. We will use a duologue where each person has such a moment. The response of actor A should be to shake their head and then look at the ceiling. That of actor B to hit his/her forehead with a closed fist. For the first go around, these reactions should be exactly as described.

A
(At the door)
Come in.

B
Thanks.

A
You are?

B

I work with Jim. Listen, I got a call—he had been hit by a car crossing Roosevelt Ave. ★

(Actor A takes the arrow.)

I didn't want to phone so I came over.

A

Ummm. That's… caring of you, very responsible, but… he's in the kitchen doing a stir fry.

(No reaction.)

Jim is in the kitchen. ★

(Actor B takes the arrow.)

You could stay if you want, he makes way too much.

COACHING

Insist on the reaction described, no more, no less. After each student's exercise, say "believable" or "unbelievable," no more is necessary. When everyone has worked, do the exercise again with the actor providing their own reaction, but still at the starred moments. *If these reactions are not visible enough, ask for a repetition.* Do the same if they are visible but not believable. I would suggest a third go-round asking for a new and different reaction at the starred moment. When these repetitions are finished, you might remind them that, obviously, you are not suggesting that all reactions be sizable, you are simply giving permission to go further when character and situation allow it.

USAGE

In the next exercise, the student finds the moment when they "take the arrow" and reacts (we hope) spontaneously at that moment. One each, please.

Exercise

A

Look, I know you hate my guts. It's not exactly impossible to tell, the way you react when I walk in a room. Several people have mentioned it to me. Your mother for instance. On the other hand, I don't think you know I stole your watch. I don't know why. I'll leave it on the table.

B

Actually, I saw you do it. I got it on the street for nine bucks and change. I told your mother just for the hell of it. And, by the way, the other night you didn't lose your car keys. They're at the bottom of Justine's pool. How about some coffee?

Coaching

Insist on one larger reaction apiece. There can, of course, be other reactions, but only once does the actor "take the arrow." You've already set the terms of sufficient size plus believability, so you can comment on either. Not satisfied. Ask them to repeat. Don't let go of the exercise 'til everyone has succeeded. *Repetition is not a punishment, it's an opportunity.* That's why rehearsal is at least a month long. An actor in trouble with the exercise? Suggest throwing something (not at anybody) or stamping a foot, shaking your hands at the heavens or whatever. The experience needed is the reaction of some size. They must give themselves permission, thus discovering the floor does not give way beneath them, nor does Stanislavski rise from the dead. *Believability can be created at any size, it does not reside exclusively in the world of miniatures.* Let's do one more. This one is a reaction without gesture. Please don't tell anyone I actually say such things to actors but the solution is "making a face." I didn't actually write that... You're seeing things. One each, please.

Exercise
  A
  So my father had this thing on his desk, a spindle... kind of like a spike on a base. He would spear papers on it... stuff he needed to keep. His brother was blind, okay, he comes in one day, leans on my father's desk but he impales his hand on the spindle. He kind of runs out the door with this thing through his hand, falls down the stairs, and kills himself. I'm not making this up, okay?

  B
  Did you notice I'm eating lunch? You have possibly the worst taste of anybody I've ever met. What is the deal with you? Why would you tell me this? Plus, your elbow is in the mayonnaise. See you back at the office.

Coaching
  Face only. One each, no more. Was it visible enough to the class? Did you feel it could be justified? Remind them that the exercise of "taking the arrow" has been to allow them significant reaction in key moments. All large work is not to be disdained, but it needs to justify itself.

Set-up / Joke / Reaction

I hadn't planned on discussing the craft of comedy in these pages, but it is impossible to leave it entirely alone. I will only discuss how actors, working together, structure and deliver a laugh. *The set-up/joke/reaction trio is the spine of stage comedy.* As we are only dealing with mechanics in three or four lines, it is immaterial if it is really funny; we must simply assume it would be in a larger context. Let's understand comic structure by inventing a few lines. Let's say that two siblings have gone through the familial crisis of seeing to their father's cremation. The ashes have been returned to them in a polished cherry wood box. They sit staring at it after dinner. B, fork in hand, suddenly grabs the box, opens it, and rakes through it. A is appalled.

A
(The set-up.)
Have you gone completely berserk? What are you doing?!

B
(The joke.)
Mom wants his ring. I'm looking for his index finger.

A
(Reaction to the joke.)
The ring doesn't go on his index finger!

Usage
A little grim, but we do what we can. Now what are the mechanics of the laugh? First, the set-up. Without the set-

up, there is no laugh. It must be clear, moderately loud, and directed to the person who will deliver the joke. When B delivers the joke, it is usually, but certainly not always, played directly front. It usually has attitude and it's clearly spoken. Could be loud, could be whispered, could come after a short pause (say, two beats), or could be done quickly right off the cue, but there must be no doubt about its being clearly heard. A, taking in the line, immediately does a physical reaction (let's say slapping his/her forehead). This builds the laugh that has come right off the words "...index finger." Just as the laugh declines, A says, "The ring doesn't go on his index finger!" And this verbal reaction may get a second laugh. The trio has done its work. The first line sets the table for the laugh. The second line delivers the laugh, and the reaction builds the laugh. All three things together make the laugh. A weak, unenergetic, slow set-up will kill the laugh. The laugh line may or may not need embellishment, but it must be clear and not take so long that the audience gets ahead of the laugh (i.e., sees it coming). The reaction to the laugh line-usually amazement, annoyance, or wild confusion-builds the laugh. Teamwork. The laugh doesn't simply belong to the moment the "funny" thing is said. Let's do it.

A
Have you gone completely berserk? What are you doing?!

B
Mom wants his ring. I'm looking for his index finger.

A
(Slapping forehead.)
The ring doesn't go on his index finger.

COACHING

Let's suggest some blocking. B sits at a table, the box before him. A sits in a chair to his right and a bit away from the table. B picks up a fork, opens the box and begins to sort through the debris. A stands up suddenly on the line, "Have you gone completely berserk?" A then moves to the table saying, "What—are—you—doing?" in a commanding voice and separating the words. B, maintaining his focus on the box says carefully, "Mom wants his ring." B fishes out something with the fork and regards it with scientific interest, saying, "I'm looking for his index finger." He is facing front. A slaps his forehead in frustration and, throwing his arms wide, says, "The ring doesn't go on his index finger!"

Have each actor use these patterns. Now, have each class member do it again. The A's may experiment with the way they handle the set-up and then the reaction. The B's experiment with the delivery of the laugh lines. Some will put a pause between, "Mom wants his ring" and "I'm looking for his index finger." Some will play the two lines as one. Some will try it softer, some louder. Some faster, some slower. A discussion of what works and what doesn't should be encouraged. Hopefully they come out intrigued and a bit more aware of the craft of comedy.

HANDLING THE PROP

Sidekick movies. The sidekick as a narrative device is used so our hero or heroine has someone they can express things to that they can't say to anyone else. Props are the actor's sidekick, a crucial means of expression. You don't just drink tea on stage, the *way* you drink the tea expresses just how pissed off you are. Let's stop here for a moment and do an exercise. We will need a teapot, cup, saucer, sugar bowl and spoon. During the exercise, pour tea, put in sugar, stir, drink, return cup to saucer.

A
(Sitting at a table.)
A boss is a boss. They call, you come. Oak door, carved. Too eminent to have a name plate. I go in, he's in trunks and sneakers stripped to the waist, wearing boxing gloves, hitting a heavy bag hung to the right of his desk. "Oh," he says, "It's you. Joan is off today and I know you're preparing the Kleenex presentation, but would you mind running down and getting me a decaf soy latte with extra whipped cream?" "Certainly Jack, my pleasure, and I went out, emptied my desk, and left.

USAGE
The point of the exercise is to transfer interior states to the way the props are used.

COACHING
Because this is a demonstration as much as an exercise, you needn't have everyone perform it. Three actors each

doing the piece three times would be sufficient. If you wish to use it as a full class exercise, I would have each actor do only two of the three states.

First point out how the props become the expression of the state. It is an excellent lesson for those who watch how the actor makes visible a feeling. If it is film, the camera can be twelve inches from the actor and understand the interior life from a glint in the eye. On stage the need to make inner work visible creates a different set of acting problems. Then ask those who watch to think of the handling of the objects. How did that, specifically, reveal feeling? When an actor is in some way unsuccessful with the exercise, what went wrong? Obviously, if the actor were to rehearse this scene for four weeks, it would be more secure and have better flow and details. That is unimportant for the moment to our understanding. Now let's do a class-wide exercise building on this beginning. Now we are interested in using the prop to punctuate the speech.

USAGE

There would be a long list of moments where what we do with the preparing and drinking of the tea will assist the presentation of the text. Here is a very limited list to explain the point of the exercise.
1. "A boss is a boss." Picks up cup. Cup becomes the boss.
2. "...hitting a heave bag." Taps table with spoon.
3. "...getting me a decaf soy latte with extra whipped cream." Having poured, added sugar and stirred, the actor drops the spoon from a height.
4. "...emptied my desk..." Drinks last of tea.
5. "...and left." Turns cup upside down on saucer.

What we want to achieve now is to combine the character's attitude or inner state and its effect on the props, with the use of the props to punctuate the story. The punctuation could be, and probably should be, simple. It might be only the click of the teacup hitting the saucer at the end of the

199

story, or it could have several elements as in the illustration numbered above. In any case, let's use the same speech and the idea of punctuation.

COACHING

In comedy, the punctuation might be complex and in drama simple. Remind the students that the actor may aggressively use the prop to serve the narrative or simply allow it to provide a behavioral background. In this exercise, we are working on the former. The first measure of this exercise is whether the actor understands the idea of punctuation with props. That will be success enough in the exercise. Now let's do the same speech one more time as the aforementioned "behavioral background." This time, drinking tea is simply "drinking tea." It's not a creative act; it carries no particular weight; it's simply pouring and drinking tea while the story is told. When this third iteration is finished, you should recap by restating these three ways of using the prop:
1. Simply as behavioral background.
2. As expressions of the inner state.
3. As punctuation for the text (this includes their becoming metaphors as in turning the cup face down after the final line.)

In the "behavioral background" version we just did, the actors may find it difficult now to make the props take a secondary role. It is, however, another necessary skill.

DETAIL

Detail is one of the major components of good acting. It's the tasty stew of the little things that provide thought process, depth, variety, emphasis, and internal life to the performance. Almost all the craft described here contributes to that end. I include it as a category only to impress on the student actor the necessity of it's presence. Almost all the combo exercises at the end of the book make this same point. Let's simply do one speech.

USAGE

For the sake of opening a door on this necessity in good acting, we will have each actor do the speech three times, each time adding a new layer of detail. The first time through after learning the speech, we will add physical detail.

A

So I was on I-25, you know, on the way to Albuquerque and it was icy after the storm. Scared me. This guy on a hog, a Harley, comes barreling past me and cuts in front. I honked. I shouldn't have honked. He looks back and then looses control, the bike 360's, tips, and the guy slides, separates from the cycle and hits a pole. Metal pole on this mileage sign and it... it severs his arm. I see his arm in my rearview sliding across the highway. Listen, would it be alright if I had a cup of coffee?

USAGE

Have the actor simply say the speech once, straight forwardly, not loading upon it. Now add a physical activity.

This activity should be common place: picks up some spilled change, takes a sliver out of his/her hand, tries to make a house of cards, etc. This activity should take up the better part of the speech.

Coaching

The activity may be done in pauses or throughout. It may take place and be completed, or be abandoned in the middle. The activity may seem common place or be imbued with the actors' feeling. You might tell the actor that the activity should have several parts. It's not just picking up a pencil and putting it down. Sharpening a pencil with a pen knife would be better. Have all the actors do the speech with this first layer. It's best, of course, if the activity parses the speech rather than just existing. That, for instance, pauses in the activity coincide with an emotional moment, or the house or cards falls when the motorcycle rider does. Such moments where the activity deepens the speech should be complimented. Now let's add another layer of detail. Let's make use of silence.

Usage

We will retain the activity and add two silences, each of three beats (a thousand one, a thousand two, a thousand three). Each actor should place these two silences where they help the internal life. The activity can be continued during these silences or stopped during them. Actor's choice. Let's start another round of the same exercise with both layers.

Coaching

This really isn't a matter of right or wrong. The only thing the teacher might address is if the place chosen seems in some way to lack impact. Otherwise, we should just thank the actors and move on to the third layer.

Usage

Yes, we're going to do one more round with the same speech, keeping the activity and the silence. This time, we'll

add the giving and taking of the eyes. The actor will only look directly at the viewer twice, and that for only the length of one sentence. The rest of the time, the actor will look elsewhere, at the activity, the floor, the ceiling, wherever. This is the third layer.
1. The activity
2. Two silences of three beats each
3. Focus on the viewers only twice. Each for one sentence. When those two direct looks are is actor's choice.

Good. Now let's present the speech with our three layers, each layer providing (our real subject) details.

COACHING

At this point, the teacher watches without comment unless one of the three layers is forgotten or the simple rules of the exercise breached. It is at the end of the final round that the discussion should return to "details." The activity is, as a whole, a detail. The giving and taking of the eyes are details. These details, which reveal inner state, are what enrich acting. Over the course of the play, when activity is fully combined with stillness and simplicity in a way that reveals the text, they give us acting and storytelling we never forget. There could be many different layers; this exercise is simply to illustrate for the actor the necessity and impact of detail.

Doing Nothing

In a certain sense, nothing exists without its opposite, no fast without slow, no still without movement. For the moment, we won't worry about that (the next technique will). Right now, we're just going to experience "still." "Still" can be frightening to the actor because of a deep sense that a lot of us have that we're not enough. We aren't smart enough, pretty enough, interesting enough. Onstage, if we don't distract those watching us, they will find us out. Being still sets off our alarms. Actually, the opposite is true, when we are still the audience fully takes in our complete difference from anyone else they've ever seen. They truly, for the first time, see us. And they're fascinated. They also, by the way, recognize it as brave. Our stillness, once accepted by the watchers, puts a laser focus on the text. It pops it out. Let's experiment with a high level of movement and then complete stillness with the same piece of text.

A
I guess I was afraid. I couldn't even recognize it, didn't let myself feel it as first. I mean, I'd done some pretty crazy stuff, traveled in some pretty dangerous places, walked alone on some dark nights, but I never felt this before. I turned around there's a coiled snaked on the wall and it rises straight up, right on eye level with me. And we both... just stay there. Six inches apart. That was pure fear. Unadulterated.

Usage
Let's begin with an activity that continues throughout the text. Packing a suitcase perhaps, or washing dishes or

an exercise regimen. Whatever is selected, the actor should try to spend the majority of time in motion. After each class member has completed the exercise in this way, they should do it again, but this time sitting in a chair without gesture (none). They can move their head, but nothing else.

COACHING

When round one (moving) and round two (still) are completed, you should initiate a discussion of what the still version accomplishes. What are its virtues? Obviously, you are not suggesting it is necessarily superior, but we are trying to discuss the values of "still." Among them, naturally, is a protection and clarifying of the text. You might mention that when dealing with a complex text or profoundly emotional state stillness is often a great help. At these times, the distraction of movement can be just that, a distraction. Stillness also seems to free emotion in many actors. It's as if the emotion says, "You seem pretty busy here and there's no room for me, so give me a call if I'd be useful." Emotion often needs the room stillness provides, to flood the actor's being. A third value is the concentration that stillness provides which can be laser sharp. Now having discussed what the actors saw in their classmates' work, let's do one more entirely still exercise.

EXERCISE

A

When I saw him walk in front of the train my heart stopped. He was so calm, almost as if he was out for a stroll. He turned and waved to me and smiled and then walked out on the tracks. You couldn't hear the sounds of the train hitting him because of its own racket. It just lifted him up and then he was on the side of the train I couldn't see. And then there was another sound and it was me screaming though I didn't realize at the time. You asked what happened. That's what happened.

Usage

As still as possible. If there is slight movement—hands folding, a shift of position, a looking down and back up, that's fine.

Coaching

There are some speeches that because of their content require little of the actor except a present heart. The speech will do the work if left unadorned. This, we are going to posit, is one. The actor needs to personalize (find some parallel or something that simply provokes a like emotion), but other than that stillness will be enough. The teacher need only insist on the stillness. It should be clear enough that the stillness serves. Now we are going to still/movement/still and work on the mixing stillness and movement.

*This exercise should follow or precede still/movement/still in a class context.

The False Exit

This one must be easily as old as the bard or anon. The description is easy. An actor or actress turns to leave the room, the country, or, in science fiction, the universe. Before getting to the door, the border, or the teleportation device, something internal or external interrupts the exit and the person exiting turns back for a final look, line, or the dastardly use of their nuclear laser side arm. It was, you see, a false exit. Let's do it for the look.

Usage

It would be helpful to these exercises if the room has a door frame or rolling door. If not, the class can center on and make use of the door by which they entered the room.

Exercise

(A and B sit on a soft or a mock sofa made up a chairs.)

A

Yes, you can be sure you've made yourself clear.

(Rises and moves behind sofa.)

It's one of your nicest qualities, clarity. I get it.

(Starts for door.)

Goodbye.
(Just before reaching the door, he or she stops, turns back, gives B a long look, then turns and exits, slamming the door.)

COACHING
There needs to be a thought process that turns them back and a thought process as they take the final look. When they finally make the exit, the move should be decisive and not tentative. In this next exercise, we'll simply add a line on the turn back.
A
Yes, you can be sure you've made yourself clear.

(Rises and moves behind sofa.)

It's one of your nicest qualities, clarity. I get it.

(Starts for door.)

Goodbye.

(Turns back before reaching door.)

You never were any good as an actor/actress, by the way.

(Turns and exits, slamming door.)

COACHING
As with most technique, what makes it work is thought process and the circumstances. Let's do it once more, giving the turn back an action rather than a look or a line.

EXERCISE
A
Yes, you can be sure you've made yourself clear.

(Rises and moves behind sofa.)

It's one of your nicest qualities, clarity. I get it.

(Starts for door.)

Goodbye.

(Turns back and zaps B with a nuclear laser side arm. Waits 'til B collapses. Turns and exits, slamming door.)

USAGE

A nice touch is if the actor gets all the way to the door, opens it, then turns back and gives look, line, or business. Exits and closes door. You might try that on this final exercise. The actor begins on the sofa and uses the lines for a false and then real exit. The reason for the turn back is up to the actor.

EXERCISE
A
(Sitting on sofa with B.)
I'm glad I got to see you. You're doing well; I hoped you would be. I had it in my mind there might be something else to do or say, but I was always a hopeless optimist. If you don't mind, call Jenny and tell her I was in town. Or don't. I'm glad to see you've still got some of my furniture.

USAGE

You can have some fun by making it a double false exit. Two "turnbacks" in other words. You might also use the talking walk-off where the actor keeps speaking even after they have left the room. In that case, you may leave the door open when you exit. You can even use the surprise return where the actor exits, closes the door, then re-opens it for a final look or line, and then closes it again to complete the exit. In any case, this exercise is actor's choice as long as it contains some version of the false exit.

COACHING

Accept all variations and enjoy them. You might even ask each actor to do it twice each time, showing a new variation.

You can assure them that they'll find some use for this in performance. Every living actor with a career has.

Sounds

For the actor, there are sounds to be made besides talking. Perhaps the most famous and significant sound ever made by an actor is Nora, at the end of *A Doll's House*, closing the door as she leaves. We may be lucky enough to run across something like that in our career, but there are smaller moments to be made. The sound of a water glass being put down, which punctuates an important moment. The sound of a letter being torn when a love is sundered. The sound of a set of keys being thrown against a wall in anger. The sound of clapping hands as an actor applauds another ironically. Sometimes, such moments are written into the text, but usually they are the spontaneous or planned work of the actor. Any exercise we try is simply to get the actor thinking of the non-verbal possibilities. Let's see what the actor can create in a given situation. We'll need props. Perhaps the teacher can provide us with a dinner set up for two (we can do it without the food). Two plates, two cups and saucers, sugar bowl, creamer, silverware, salt and pepper shakers, napkins, and, for fun, a table bell to summon a servant.

A
How is the salmon?

B
Excellent, first rate. I would have expected no less. The table setting is art, that's you all over.

A
Well, I know you well enough to know what gives you pleasure.

B
Yes, you do actually. You know, your brother said I should beware.

A
Ah, did he?

B
He said you probably invited me here to poison me.

A
That being the case. Should you be eating?

B
I have confidence in you, you see.

A
Oh dear. Misplaced. You'll suffer excruciating pain within the minute.

B
Really?

A
Really. I wish you a bon voyage.

(B creates a final sound as good as Nora's.)

USAGE

The actors should create a soundscore to accompany the scene. Not too much now. Better to be a bit austere than to overdo it. The final sound, of course, should be wonderful. No death throes, please.

COACHING

Again, we are creating awareness of the idea. Hopefully the actors have fun and it opens a door for them. You can request less or more, but there is no real way to do this *in*correctly. Well, perhaps if the work is too exaggerated. Let's do one more.

USAGE

In this second exercise, the soundscore should be created with the only props used being common place things in their pocket or on their bodies. This time, there is no furniture (harder). This time, the sounds are created by the feet, hands clapping, fingers snapping, whistling, etc. In addition, they may use whatever they are carrying. The exercise takes place outdoors in a field. This I, by the way, harder for the actor than the previous exercise.

EXERCISE

A
Ummm. Let me put it to you this way. We're lost.

B
You're kidding.

A
No, I don't think I'm kidding.

B
I thought you were the master woodsman? I can't believe this. I'm freezing by the way. Great, I'm going to die in a lean-to on my birthday.

A
Melodrama. We have matches, I can make shelter, we have food.

B
Three cans of Boston baked beans? You are… scaring me. I don't even like woods. It's claustrophobic, it's wet, stuff scratches you. Get me out of here.

A
You're freaked. That surprises me. I've never seen you freak. I'm going to give you your birthday present.

B
What?!

A
We're not lost, I was kidding.

Usage

The class may find themselves short of sound-making behavior. I often ask them for a list of ten sounds that could be used before the exercise begins.

Coaching

Working in open space is always good for the actors. With so many cinematic plays with thirty locations, the actor often finds themselves on a basically empty stage. Remind them to take a few moments to visualize their surroundings. Most actors have backpacks and these can be used in the scene. Are the sounds in the actor driven soundscore useful to the moment or extraneous? Is it overused? Can you point out moments when it works well? Do they, additionally, use the space in an interesting way? The tougher problems of working in open space are worth touching on, though I do not address them in this book. If actors are having problems, send them off to plan the sounds. This doesn't have to *be* spontaneous, it only has to *look* spontaneous. When someone does it well, try to articulate why it worked. Usually, it is contextual, the actor sound clarifies psychology, the use is believable, and the sound enriches the text.

The Double Take

All right, I'm doing this for fun, but actors have been doing this forever. Some say it originated in Burlesque. I'm going to guess it originated with Aristophanes. The actor will find a use for it. Every actor should know how to tango and every actor should know the double take.

Usage
Moments of amazement.

Coaching
Here's how to do it. The actor is in downtown Tulsa. Before he crosses the street, he looks to his left, but looks immediately back to center because there are no cars. It suddenly strikes him that though there are no cars, there was something else! He turns his head slowly back to check if he saw what he thought he saw. Yes, there is a charging elephant! He now looks back to center with a look of terrified amazement. That's it.

The double take with a reaction to what he saw thrown in. Actually, the look back can also be fast as lightning (the look that sees the elephant). This depends on the actor's feeling about what he sees. Let's review the physical only. A look to left or right (normal, nothing unusual). The look goes back to center (the actor hasn't registered anything amazing). A sudden, quick look back in the direction of the first look (did he actually see an elephant?). Back to center, amazed. (Yes, there is an elephant, and it's lavender!)

EXERCISE
A
So, this is the cafeteria. The main course kind of sucks but the desserts are terrific.

(Hears something and looks to his right. Looks back to center.)

Anyway...

(Suddenly looks back to right, startled. He has seen a naked waiter with a meat cleaver. Looks back center.)

Okay, this is a little unusual.

COACHING
This is truly both a matter of mechanics and inner life. The first look (left or right) is a normal glance, pretty much without affect. The look back center is the same. All is as it should be. When the actor looks back, right or left, it has the confused necessity of confirming something astounding the brain has finally registered. When the elephant or naked waiter is actually there, there is true amazement. The look back to center is the actor trying to process that the impossible has been seen. I often treat this as choreography. I stand in front of the class and call out the units of action that they do. Look left, look back center, look suddenly left, look back center amazed. After they do this in unison, say three times, I proceed to the scripted exercises.

EXERCISE
A
So, that's the way they say Jim died. They never found the body.

(Double take, because here comes Jim.)

I don't see that.

Coaching

There are two areas of focus. The mechanics of the take. Everybody needs to get that right. Often the second look that takes in the elephant isn't fast enough. The second area to be watched and criticized is the interior life that accompanies the double take. Does the actor have a reason to glance left? Is the return to center normal and offhand? Is the second look energized and the stakes high? Is the second return to center truly amazed? It is possible also to conclude the double take the moment the actor sees the elephant and is dumbfounded. In that case, the second look back to center is cut. Have the actors re-do the exercise cutting the last look center. Done.

Giving and Taking the Eyes

The eyes. Ah yes, the windows of the soul, the display case of the actor's emotion. However, the eyes are also political, sexual, manipulative, and work as a symbiology of dominance and submission. Geishas study the use and impact of the eyes for years. In American business, direct eye contact implies a trustworthy person. In flirtation, the holding of eye contact beyond a few seconds signals mutual interest. In circumstances where we are in the presence of "authority," we maintain eye contact to signal our interest or look down to symbolize submission. There are times when our eyes are working intuitively and other times when we use them to signal. It is in this second area that our interest lies. Thus the exercise, the giving and taking of the eyes.

More specifically, when and for how long do we hold another's gaze? Why? In almost every social situation, there are cultural norms related to eye contact. *There are also many reasons why we avoid the other's gaze. On stage, this negotiation can become highly theatrical.* I hold your gaze steadily; when I look away, I make a point. The reverse would also signify. In our work, we cannot really tell the actor whether to give or take because it is too personal and psychologically complex. We can, however, remind them that the length they hold another's eyes or avoid them signifies and when we move from holding to looking away makes a point.

Exercise
 A
  I know you've been dreading this moment. Certainly scares me. All right, here we go. *I love you.* I apologize but there's no getting away from it. I

wasn't going to tell you… but that's ridiculous. *Now, you're told.*

USAGE

The actor/actress should only make eye contact with the listening partner on the two italicized lines. Where is the actor looking the rest of the time? At his hands, the ceiling, the floor… wherever his thought process carries him. Equally good, of course, is behavior. The cleaning of glasses, the drinking of coffee, the cutting of fingernails. Any common task will provide a focal point away from the other actor.

COACHING

As the "thigh bone is connected to the leg bone," so the eyes are connected to the heart and the given circumstances. With this exercise (as with others), you may want to talk for a minute about this particular love. Why is the person speaking not making direct eye contact? If you prefer not to take the time to elicit it from the group, you could use this: A has proposed to B numerous times, and all in vain. B doesn't want to marry until they finish graduate school (or some such). B has forbidden A to speak romantically for a month. Coach A to make the avoidance of B's eyes psychologically apt. The phrase "I don't believe it yet" may be all that's necessary. It's useful to point out that if the actor's focus is away from B and making eye contact means a definite turn it may have more impact. After all present have tried the exercise, you might ask them to try it again and pick two different moments for the eye contact. Then ask the other class members how it changes the meaning.

EXERCISE

A
I didn't think you'd come back.

B
Sorry, my temper is a cross to bear.

A
I shouldn't have said that, not that way.

B
Why do we do this?

A
Can we not talk about it?

B
No, we can't "not" talk about it.

A
I need to be treated differently, do you get that?

B
And you, just to be blunt, need to watch your mouth.

A
There's lasagna left.

B
Lasagna's fine.

USAGE

The exercise should be repeated twice. The first time A makes eye contact only once and B twice. The next time that is exactly reversed. When the actors know the lines, the choice of where to make eye contact may be spontaneous. It need not be planned.

COACHING

Demand that the moments of eye contact be clear. On film, you could be looking only very slightly down, then raise your eyes to your partner, and it would read as extravagant. On stage, the change of focus needs to be a little stronger. Some actors mask their eyes by keeping their focus always slightly below their partner's eyes. You may need to ask them to lift their chins so that their eyes "read." You can tell your class that the exercises are only to sensitize them as actors to the possibilities of giving and taking away dependent on the psychology and actions being played. One last exercise.

Exercise

A

Thanks for the… gift. It's uh… it's not really necessary. Actually, it's a little awkward, we don't know each other very well. I mean, we know each other but… I'm sorry, I can't accept this. I can't.

Usage

Here, we make what is rare the looking away. The actor looks at their partner steadily and only breaks the contact for one line. The line to look away on is chosen by the actor.

Coaching

A point to make is that rarity (in this case, looking away) is very helpful in making a point clear. The actor's job is very involved with deciding which are the most important points and moments his character has. Everything said cannot be of equal importance. This is part and parcel to revealing meaning in the text. *Rarity can be a great help to both the actor and her audience.* As usual, the different moments chosen to look away by the class may, spark a conversation about meaning. Sometimes I take two students with very different takes on the exercise and have them do it one after the other. Class discussion is then directed to articulating the difference in what is revealed. It is certainly not helpful for it to become a "who-is-better" contest.

Ripples From the Big Moment

Very often when the actor plays or is confronted by "the big moment," he or she is likely to forget to have that moment sufficiently impact the moments that follow. Jill yells at Jack for forgetting to put a coaster under the breakfast honey jar and thus staining the new table. Yes, probably some much larger issue is driving Jill, but we're not going to get into that, because we'd have to write the play. What we're interested in is that actors (sometimes experienced ones) forget to carry over their reaction to their own outburst to the next several lines. She has the outburst and then it's as if it never existed. Sadly, I've seen it a hundred times (well, actually a thousand.) Why, you say, would an actor make such a rookie mistake? Yes, because they aren't sufficiently inside the role and situation. And you know what? More often than not, they won't be. Would that it were otherwise, but both in class and in production, you need immediate ways to rectify the problem and it would take a year (or an eternity) to redirect the emotional and belief structure of that actor so that they better play "as if" and truly make internal use of the given circumstances. Failing the time or rare talent that could handle the problem, I try to make them aware of where the big moment is (hopefully they will identify it in future) and understand their responsibility to the moments that follow. This technique is actually part of the actor's dramaturgy. Okay, what is a big moment? That's completely situational, so let's keep it simple and say when the actor is wildly angry and loud, or weeps, or is slapped or pushed, or intentionally breaks a glass, or reveals something powerfully emotional from their past, or has to play the "Benny, I'm pregnant" moment. You get the idea. Let's proceed to an exercise.

Usage

This work is bound to be a bit sketchy because our six or eight line exercise can't really provide the internal build or surrounding circumstances so I'll give a brief background and make the "big moment" physical.

Coaching

Tell them before the exercise that you are merely trying to sensitize them to identifying a big moment and understanding their responsibility to the moments that follow. *In other words, the technique is to see the problems and begin working on the solution. The technique does not provide the solution. Forewarned is forearmed.*

Exercise Background

Actor A has information that the company he/she works for has been cooking the books. Her direct superior wants her to withhold this information from the press until the company stabilizes its situation with guaranteed loans. Actor B is A's direct superior.

A
I'm sorry, I'm going to the press this afternoon.

B
For the sake of this truth, this abstraction, you'd put seventeen hundred people out of work?

A
The company is guilty of fiscal irresponsibility, fraud, quality control that endangers consumers, and has fired a third of the work force under false pretenses. I will go to the press with this "abstraction," yes.

(A Rises.)
(B is furious. Grabs A roughly by the arm and forcibly sits him/her.)

B
You will sit down and you will shut up!

A
Excuse me.

B
Shut up!!!

★ *This is the big moment. The remainder of the scene is affected by its ripples.*

A
I think it would be better if you moved out of the way and let me leave.

B
That was… that was unnecessary. I apologize for losing my temper.

A
I have a press conference at 3 pm, this is a breakdown of the salient points I intend to make.

(A hands B a file.)

B
You are no longer in our employ. You are now simply a disgruntled ex-employee.

A
This stuff could have been fixed. Now it's criminal behavior.
(A leaves. B sits.)

Usage

The scene is long enough, it should be given to the actors overnight before it is performed.

Coaching

The teachable part of the exercise is after B roughly handles A and then yells at him/her. *The key is that both actors are shaken by the "big moment" and remain so until the end of the scene.* There is no easy recovery from such a moment and it colors the acting until A's exit. There are many colors possible: surprise, regret, physical pain, the sense of having made a huge mistake, fear, embarrassment, anger, a sense of loss, etc.

The teacher's position is to make sure that ripples from the big moment are present thereafter, that the big moment doesn't simply occur and then the acting goes on as if it never happened. The teacher must assist the actors in understanding and communicating the impact of the moment right through the final line. First the actor must recognize the big moment and then allow its impact in the aftermath. Let's try one more exercise.

Usage

In this exercise, the actor must identify the moment (fairly obvious) and then deal with the ripples. The "ripples," as has been previously noted, are the carryover of feelings and attitudes from the big moment. The length of the carryover is situational, but almost invariably it's more than a couple of lines.

Exercise

Background

A and B are roommates. Let's say this is their second year of sharing the same space. They are also friends. A particularly feels there is mutual trust. When the exercise opens, B is about to go out. He/she starts for the door.

A
You dropped something.

B
I'll get it.

A
(Bending over.)
Got it.

(A moment.)

This is my mother's engagement ring.

B
Yeah. Right. I found it on the floor...

(Could be true, could be false. Actor's choice.)

A
I keep it in a drawer.

B
Maybe got caught when you took something out.

A
You're stealing from me.

B
I can't...
(Actor must know what the end of the sentence is.)

I found it on the floor.

A
Why would you steal from me?

B
How am I supposed to answer that?

(Pause. Who knows what each is thinking?)

A
I have to go to class *(or work)*.

B
Me too. We're both late.

A
We need eggs.

B
I'll pick them up.

A
And pepper.

(They look at each other. B leaves.)

COACHING
It could easily be played that either "this is my mother's engagement ring" or "you're stealing from me" could be the big moment. In any case, the rest of the scene is played under its shadow. Whichever is chosen, the teacher might discuss with the actors, prior to performance, what the range of their feelings and attitudes might be that constitute the ripple. When the exercise is played, the coaching switches to an analysis of whether or not the ripples were evident and believable. Very often, the actors will need a couple of tries to accomplish some part of the task. I'm going to leave this category after two exercises, not because it doesn't deserve more, but because the emotional necessities almost take it out of the craft category. What is craft is the recognition that there is internal work to be done afterward.

Course Structures

Outline for Teaching Beginning Craft

The Verbal
    Spreading the Line   Pg 65
    Framing the Line   Pg 73
    Breaking Up the Line   Pg 69
    The Cut Line   Pg 84
    The Pause   Pg 128

The Rhythm
    The Run On Sentence   Pg 59
    Rhythm Blocks   Pg 113
    Shared Rhythm   Pg 121
    The Quick Part   Pg 125
    The Slow Part   Pg 128
    Beats as Rhythm   Pg 139
    The Build   Pg 143
    Lay On / Lay Off   Pg 148

The Physical
    Physicalizing the Transition   Pg 17
    Focus Points   Pg 21
    Still / Movement / Still   Pg 29
    Taking the Arrow   Pg 191
    The Helicopter   Pg 56

Doing Things
    Behavior   Pg 154
    Handling the Prop   Pg 198
    Doing Nothing   Pg 198
    Set-Up / Joke / Reaction   Pg 204
    The False Exit   Pg 207
    The Double Take   Pg 215

Outline for Teaching Advanced Craft

The Verbal
    Throwing the Line Away   Pg 76
    The Greater Overlap   Pg 90
    The Lesser Overlap   Pg 93
    Lifting   Pg 96
    Unwritten Interjection   Pg 100
    Closing it Down   Pg 79
    Flat   Pg 105

The Rhythm Review
    Rhythm Blocks   Pg 116
    Shared Rhythm   Pg 121
    The Quick Part   Pg 125

The Physical
    Props in Eight   Pg 176
    Three Gestures   Pg 53
    Changing Architecture   Pg 42
    Intuitive and Intentional Gestures   Pg 47
    Hold the Gesture, Control the Drop Pg 51
    Choreographing Behavior   Pg 182
    Focus Points   Pg 21

Doing Things
    Clean and Dirty   Pg 160
    Torque   Pg 25
    The Eyes   Pg 218
    Ripples from the Big Moment   Pg 222
    Vacillation   Pg 34

If Only One Craft Course is Taught

The Verbal
    Cut Lines   Pg 84
    Closing it Down   Pg 79
    Flat   Pg 105
    Throwing the Line Away   Pg 76
    Lifting   Pg 96
    Spreading the Line   Pg 65

The Rhythm
    The Run On   Pg 59
    Rhythm Blocks   Pg 113
    The Quick Part   Pg 121
    The Pause   Pg 128
    Lay On / Lay Off   Pg 148

The Physical
    Changing Focus   Pg 21
    Still / Movement / Still   Pg 29
    Torque   Pg 25
    Intuitive and Intentional Gesture   Pg 47
    Changing Architecture   Pg 42

Doing Things
    Clean and Dirty   Pg 160
    Handling the Prop   Pg 198
    Doing Nothing   Pg 204
    Taking the Arrow   Pg 191

    or, make your own . . .

ACTING CRAFT FOR HIGH SCHOOLS

THE VERBAL
    Spreading the Line   Pg 65
    Breaking the Line   Pg 69
    Throwing the Line Away   Pg 76
    Lifting   Pg 96
    Closing it Down   Pg 79

THE RHYTHM
    Rhythm Blocks   Pg 113
    Shared Rhythm   Pg 121
    The Quick Part   Pg 125
    The Pause   Pg 128

THE PHYSICAL
    Physicalizing the Transition   Pg 17
    Focus Points   Pg 21
    Vacillation   Pg 34
    The Helicopter   Pg 56

DOING THINGS
    Behavior   Pg 154
    Clean and Dirty   Pg 160
    Taking the Arrow   Pg 191
    Handling the Prop   Pg 198
    The Eyes   Pg 218
    Detail   Pg 201

Combos

The following six speeches and duologues are used so that several techniques may be combined in one exercise. They may be interspersed in the training or used as one segment toward the end of both beginning and advanced classes. Many other exercises may be used in this way with the teacher determining the mix. It is also possible to use such mixtures as final exams. You will note that beginning techniques are sometimes used in advanced combos. This naturally assumes a beginning class has been taught. They can be replaced with others if this is not the case.

Combo Speech #1

A
Get my life together? Okay, okay but that is such a dangerously empty, look-Ma-how-much-better-I-am phrase. You want me to be you, right? Do what you do? See my deal is you have a washed out, colorless, repetitive, dead-end life. And you, you think it's "together"? Mom, that just scares me. Scares me bad. I check out your "together" and I'd rather be in a million pieces. You don't make the argument for "together" very appetizing. You are the living argument for the prosecution.

Beginning Craft Combos
1. The run-on, spreading, framing
2. Rhythm blocks, physicalizing the transition, framing
3. Clean, the quick part, breaking
4. Clean, dirty, rhythm blocks
5. The quick part, the slow part, spreading
6. Rhythm blocks, handing the prop, physicalizing the transition

Advanced Craft Combos
1. Changing focus, changing architecture
2. Small, big, changing focus
3. Small, big, changing architecture, framing
4. Vacillation, choreographed behavior
5. Big, neutral, vacillation
6. Choreographed behavior, rhythm blocks, the eyes

Combo Speech #2

Snowed in, baby. White for miles. Six foot drifts. Just you and me and how much we don't like each other. Oh, plus there's pasta and three dozens cans of sardines in soy oil. Sounds like a real party, doesn't it? You know what your worst quality is? Breathing. You wheeze when you breathe every three seconds. That's one thousand two hundred and twenty wheezes an hour. Pretty cool, huh? We're snowed in and your wheezes are all mine.

Beginning Craft Combos
1. Props in eight, physicalizing the transition, the run-on
2. The quick part, the pause, props in eight
3. Rhythm blocks, the pause, doing nothing
4. Still/movement/still, the build, the quick part
5. Behavior, the quick part, spreading
6. The build, the pause, behavior

Advanced Craft Combos
1. Lifting, the eyes, physicalizing the transition
2. Torque, neutral, the quick part
3. Changing architecture, vacillations, torque
4. The quick part, throwing away the line, closing it down
5. Rhythm blocks, choreographing behavior, throwing away the line
6. The build, changing focus, vacillation

Combo Speech #3

A
Don't give me the thousand mile stare. She's alone, she has crippling arthritis, possible dementia, she doesn't eat unless someone cooks it for her. Conclusion: she needs care. Problem: I live half a continent away, you live, maybe, six streets down. Hmmm. Where should the care come from?

B
Very nicely put. Very logical. Maybe a little sarcastic, but I'll overlook that. However, there are omissions. I'm accepted in the Peace Corps and I leave for Nigeria in six weeks.

A
Cancel.

B
Move home.

A
I have a job, you don't have a job.

B
You think the Peace Corps isn't a job?

A
I think that could be next year. It could be three years from now.

B
You're working in marketing. You glorify copper polish.

A
Enough.

B
That's right, enough.

BEGINNING CLASS COMBOS
1. The pause, the quick part, framing the line
2. The run-on sentence, the slow part, focus points
3. The false exit, taking the arrow, rhythm blocks
4. Physicalizing the transition, breaking the line, the helicopter
5. Handling the prop, run-on sentence, still/movement/still
6. Behavior, doing nothing, the quick part

ADVANCED CLASS COMBOS
1. Closing it down, three gestures, clean and dirty
2. The quick part, flat, choreographing behavior
3. Torque, vacillation, changing architecture
4. The eyes, intuitive/intentional gestures, torque
5. Props in eight, lifting, focus points
6. Hold the gesture/control drop, rhythm blocks, the eyes

Combo Speech #4

A
Woah. Okay. This is an unusual feeling. I don't want to make a big mistake here, but I think I'm happy. Focus on me, does this look like happy? 'Cause I'm thinking maybe...

B
It looks dopey. If I had to pick one of the seven dwarves, in terms of likeness, it would be Dopey. Or possibly Sneezy.

A
Sneezy is not a dwarf. And by the way, it is possible to be both happy and dopey. Or happy and incredibly perceptive.

B
Sneezy is not only a dwarf but also the best dwarf because everything in your head stops when you sneeze. When you sneeze, you have no ego, no false perspective, you are simply the sneeze. You, however, look...

A
Stop. I'm happy. I'm wildly, unreasonably happy. I exult therefore I am.

B
You know what I prefer to this conversation?

A
What?

B
Pizza. I prefer pizza to exaltation.

BEGINNING CLASS COMBOS
1.
   a. (Actor A) Behavior, helicopter, throwing the line away
   b. (Actor B) Clean, false exit, physicalizing the transition
2.
   a. (Actor A) Quick party, handling the props, the pause
   b. (Actor B) Rhythm blocks, focus points, doing nothing
3.
   a. (Actor A) Framing, the run-on, still/movement/still
   b. (Actor B) Taking the arrow, behavior, framing the line

ADVANCED CLASS COMBOS
1.
   a. (Actor A) The lesser overlap, torque, closing it down
   b. (Actor B) Vacillation, flat, changing architecture
2.
   a. (Actor A) Clean and dirty, rhythm blocks, three gestures
   b. (Actor B) Choreographing behavior, the slow part, lifting
3.
   a. (Actor A) Shared rhythm, hold gesture/control drop, torque
   b. (Actor B) Shared rhythm, props in eight, the eyes

COMBO SPEECH #5

A

I don't know, I'm just... freaking. I've got thirty, forty bucks in the bank, car payments, doctor bills, I owe six, seven people. Yeah, I got part-time work but that's minimum wage, maybe twenty hours a week. And the worst thing is, I can't see beyond it. Minimum wage stretched out to the horizon. And what am I supposed to call this, a life? I live in the most powerful nation in the world and this is what I get? Tell you what, I'll cross the line. I'll mug people, rob stores, anything like that. I won't live this way. I flat out won't.

BEGINNING CRAFT COMBOS
1. Behavior, clean, handling the prop
2. Props in eight, breaking, the slow part
3. Physicalizing the transition, dirty, the pause.
4. Rhythm blocks, doing nothing, framing
5. The quick part, the slow part, interior build
6. Still/movement/still, the pause, false exit

ADVANCED CRAFT TECHNIQUES
1. Clean and dirty, throwing away the line, actor sound
2. Still/movement/still, closing it down, intentional gesture
3. Changing architecture, vacillation, hold gesture/ control drop
4. Changing focus, quick part, torque
5. Big, neutral, the eyes
6. Lifting, changing focus, choreographing behavior

COMBO SPEECH #6

A

I don't know... what I was hoping was... listen, this was a two thousand mile drive because I couldn't leave it the way we left it. It wasn't right. Did it feel right to you? I owe you. I owe you so many different things. Probably half of what I am, if you want to add it up. Anyway, I added it up and I got in the car and I came down here. Not to start something over but to pay off. Give me a task. Treat me like Ulysses. What can I do for you?

BEGINNING CRAFT COMBOS
1.
    a. (Actor A) False exit, behavior, the slow part
    b. (Actor B) Behavior, the double take, breaking

2.
    a. (Actor A) The build, the pause, the quick part
    b. (Actor B) The build, false exit, handling the prop

3.
    a. (Actor A) Shared rhythm, clean, spreading
    b. (Actor B) Shared rhythm, dirty, framing

4.
    a. (Actor A) Still/movement/still, props in eight, the run-on
    b. (Actor B) Physicalizing the transition, the pause, the quick part

ADVANCED CRAFT COMBOS
1.
    a. (Actor A) Mini-overlap, unwritten interjection, torque

2.
   b. (Actor B) Mini-overlap, unwritten interjection, actor sound

   a. (Actor A) Actor sound, intentional gesture, small/big
   b. (Actor B) Torque, hold gesture/control drop, closing it down

3.
   a. (Actor A) The eyes, changing architecture, throwing away the line
   b. (Actor B) Vacillation, intentional gesture, neutral

Afterword

Text study first.
Belief first.
Circumstances first.
Relationships first.

Thought process always.
The action always.

Partnered by craft.
Craft making all of the above clear.

Craft provides structure and structure gives imagination and creativity point, thus revealing the text.

What could be better?

Author Biography

Mr. Jory co-founded and was the first artistic director of the Long Wharf Theatre. For thirty-one years, he was producing director of the Actor's Theatre of Louisville. He taught for a decade at the University of Washington graduate acting program and currently teaches at The Santa Fe University of Art and Design. His other books are *Tips for Actors* and *Tips for Directors*. He has been inducted into New York City's Theatre Hall of Fame. He is additionally an oft-published playwright and adaptor for the stage.